FOOD FACTS

FOR THE KITCHEN FRONT

Filled with no-nonsense war-time recipes, using pure
ingredients and simple preparation methods.
Includes valuable information on food groupings and
food factors, vital for a healthy and balanced diet.

Harper
Press

Harper*Press*
An imprint of HarperCollins*Publishers*
77–85 Fulham Palace Road
Hammersmith, London W6 8JB
www.harpercollins.co.uk

Visit our authors' blog: www.fifthestate.co.uk
Love this book? www.bookarmy.com

First published in Great Britain by Collins in 1941

This edition was first published by Harper*Press* in 2009

Copyright © HarperCollins Publishers Ltd 2009

1

A catalogue record for this book is available from the British Library

ISBN 978-0-00-731379-2

Printed and bound in Great Britain by Clays Ltd, St Ives plc

Mixed Sources
Product group from well-managed
forests and other controlled sources
www.fsc.org Cert no. SW-COC-1806
© 1996 Forest Stewardship Council

FSC is a non-profit international organisation established to promote the
responsible management of the world's forests. Products carrying the FSC
label are independently certified to assure consumers that they come
from forests that are managed to meet the social, economic and
ecological needs of present or future generations.

Find out more about HarperCollins and the environment at
www.harpercollins.co.uk/green

CONTENTS

3

A NOTE ON FOOD VALUES

ONE result of war-time feeding is that we all know something about food values. We have learnt that the foods necessary to health fall into three groups : Energy Foods, Body-building Foods, and Protective Foods.

Let us examine them briefly, with special attention to the foods that are always plentiful. Then we shall see how to eat well-balanced meals that will keep us fit.

GROUP ONE—ENERGY FOODS

Our appetite guides us to eat these foods. We need not plan for Energy Foods in our meals. When we are hungry we naturally want to eat starchy foods, fats and sugar.

Starchy Foods.—Potatoes, Bread and Cereals of all kinds satisfy our hunger and are in good supply.

Fats.—Butter, Margarine, Dripping, Bacon, etc., are still sufficient for our health. We shall not suffer in any way from eating rather less fat than formerly, provided that we eat more green vegetables.

Sugar.—Sugar, dried fruits, honey, jam and confectionery are valuable, but we should not exaggerate their importance. When we talk about " needing sugar for energy " we are inclined to overstate the case. Potatoes and bread will provide all the energy we want.

GROUP TWO—BODY-BUILDING FOODS

These, repairing the tissues, are particularly important for growing children. The main foods in this group are :

Meat, Fish, Eggs, Cheese and Milk.

We have a second line of defence in other more plentiful foods which have body-building value. They are :

Oatmeal.
Wheatmeal Bread and Flour.
Dried Peas, Beans and Lentils.
Potatoes.
Green Vegetables.

GROUP THREE—PROTECTIVE FOODS

We have never eaten enough protective foods. Even in peace-time doctors have urged us to eat more of them. They guard us against infection ; they help us to fight tiredness and depression, they keep our complexions clear. Their vitamins and essential mineral salts are indispensable in our daily diet.

It is extremely fortunate that, placed high in this group, there should be some of the foods that are plentiful throughout the year :

> Wheatmeal Bread, Oatmeal, Milk, Potatoes, Carrots, Green Vegetables (fresh or canned), Root Vegetables and Raw Salads.

In these days, when we are all beginning to concern ourselves with essentials and to discard the things that do not matter, it is necessary to remember these two facts :

1. What we *can* get is good for us.
2. A great deal of what we *cannot* get is quite unimportant.

A NOTE ON FOOD FACTORS

THOUGH we cannot expect to become scientific experts overnight, it is useful for us to learn something about calories, proteins, vitamins and mineral salts. We ought to know what they are and what they do to our bodies.

CALORIES

Calories are units of heat, which we liberate in our body-tissues when we eat Energy Foods (Starches, Fats and Sugar). Our daily caloric requirement varies according to our sex and occupation. Men need more calories than women do. People whose work calls for great physical activity need more calories than are required by sedentary workers.

PROTEINS

Food is a mixture of chemical substances, and the chemical constituent known as protein builds our muscles and tissues. Proteins are therefore particularly important to growing children.

Animal proteins are derived from the main body-building foods : Meat, Fish, Eggs, Milk and Cheese. Vegetable proteins are obtained from our " second line of defence " :

> Oatmeal.
> Wheatmeal Bread.
> Potatoes.
> Green Vegetables.
> Dried Peas, Beans and Lentils.

VITAMINS

Vitamins are food factors necessary to growth and nourishment.

Their existence was discovered when scientific research proved that artificial food mixtures (containing all the known nutritive factors in a purified state) were unable to support growth without the addition of a natural food, such as milk.

It was obvious then that natural foods must contain

7

unknown essential food factors. These are now known as vitamins. The most important are Vitamins A, B and C.

Vitamin A plays an important part in building up our resistance to infection. It is essential for the adapting of the eye to sudden changes of light. " Night blindness " may be due to a deficiency of Vitamin A.

Good sources of this vitamin are Spinach, Carrots, Cabbage, Peas and Beans. Halibut liver oil and Cod liver oil, Herrings, Margarine.

Vitamin B is essential for the correct functioning of the nervous system, which influences our digestive system.

Good sources of the vitamin are Wheatmeal Bread and Flour, Oatmeal, Vegetable Extract.

Vitamin C maintains the correct structure of the tissue of the blood-vessels. Complete absence of this vitamin from the diet leads to scurvy.

Good sources of the vitamin are Potatoes, Green Vegetables (especially raw), Root Vegetables (especially raw) and Fruit.

Vitamin values are expressed, not in ounces nor grammes but in International Units. Since our daily requirement of Vitamin A is taken as about 5,000 International Units, we may find it useful to remember that :

1 oz. Carrots contains 540 International Units of Vitamin A.
1 oz. Boiled Cabbage contains 356 International Units of Vitamin A.

By eating half a pound of carrots and four ounces of cabbage we should almost have satisfied our total daily requirement.

Our daily requirement of Vitamin B is much smaller. It is taken as 500 International Units. Here we may find it useful to remember that :

1 oz. Oatmeal contains 92 International Units of Vitamin B.
1 oz. Wheatmeal Bread contains 28 International Units of Vitamin B.

By eating four ounces of oatmeal and four ounces of wheatmeal bread we should again be very near the figure of our total daily requirement.

Our daily requirement of Vitamin C is taken as 1,250 International Units.

Here we may find it useful to remember that :

1 oz. Potatoes contains from 105-140 International Units of Vitamin C.

1 oz. Boiled Cabbage contains 95 International Units of Vitamin C.

By eating half a pound of potatoes and a quarter of a pound of cabbage we can satisfy our total daily requirement of Vitamin C.

MINERAL SALTS

Iron and Calcium.—We should be careful to guard against a deficiency of Iron in our foods. Iron is an element of great importance in the body, specially to women and girls, who need it to safeguard them against tiredness and anæmia.

Good sources of Iron are Wheatmeal Bread, Oatmeal, Watercress and Spinach.

Calcium is necessary to our bodies for building bones and teeth. This naturally means that it is of great importance to growing children, to expectant and nursing mothers.

Good sources of Calcium are Milk and Green Vegetables.

VEGETABLES

It was once said that English cooking demanded a Society for the Prevention of Cruelty to Vegetables. But now we no longer regard them as a mere accompaniment to a meat dish—a food to be cooked in water and served haphazardly. We are learning to value them highly and cook them well.

We can produce enough vegetables in our country to feed the whole nation. Last year saw our production enormously increased by the Dig for Victory Campaign. This year, as the diggers grow more numerous and more experienced, we shall increase it still further.

We recognise the importance of vegetables as a Protective Food. We know that some (potatoes for example) are good Energy Food also.

Not only are they valuable food, but properly cooked or attractively served raw, vegetables are delicious, full of variety, and capable of being used in a number of different ways.

A salad can be as pretty as a bunch of flowers, yet do you as much good as a steak and kidney pudding. Even if you like a meat and vegetable meal best, don't forget that you can feed well from a course of vegetables alone. Or, if you are near the end of your meat ration, an extra vegetable will transform it into a substantial meal.

The main thing to remember in cooking vegetables is to bring them to table as near their normal selves, and with as much of their natural goodness as possible. Cook them in a steamer if you can ; they will retain more flavour.

Wash all green vegetables thoroughly and soak them in cold water with a teaspoon of salt for not more than half an hour. Then shred them finely. If you are going to " boil " them, go easy with the water. Put them into a saucepan with *not more* than a teacupful of boiling water and a pinch of salt. If you can, add a fleck of margarine or cooking fat on top, though in these rationed days you may not be able to spare it.

Replace the lid and boil steadily for 10-15 minutes, shaking the pan to keep the vegetables clear. Drain the vegetables well and serve them hot. Any stock that remains should be strained off and used for gravy or soup.

Use the outside leaves of green vegetables. Shred them

and put them into soup, or add them shredded to a
hot-pot.

For root vegetables—carrots, turnips, swedes, etc.—the
most important thing to remember is to scrape or peel
them lightly, taking as little off the edible parts as possible.
Steam them if you can, boil them in a very little salted
water if you can't. They are good, too, baked round the
joint or in a very little water in a dish in the oven. The
only exception to this rule is beetroot (see p. 15).

ARTICHOKES (Jerusalem)

These are good winter vegetables, rarely used as much
as they might be.

If the artichokes are dipped in very hot water prior to
peeling, the skin scrapes off very easily, and with little
waste. Place them immediately into cold water to which
a little vinegar has been added, to save them from
discolouring.

They can then be steamed, or boiled in a little salted
water. For a more nourishing dish, cook them in sufficient
boiling milk and water, in equal quantities, to just cover,
add a pinch of salt and cook steadily for 15-20 minutes
with the lid on the saucepan. Remove the vegetables and
thicken the stock as described on page 115. Then replace
the artichokes in the sauce, heat up and serve.

ARTICHOKE SOUP

1 pint vegetable boilings or water.	1 oz. cooking fat or margarine.
½ pint milk.	1½ lb. artichokes.
	A little chopped spring onion.
Seasoning of pepper and salt.	

Peel and slice the artichokes as above and chop the
onion. Toss the vegetables in the melted fat, lid on the
pan, until the fat is absorbed and the flavours are well
drawn. Pour on the water or vegetable liquor, add a
pinch of salt, replace the lid and allow to simmer for half
an hour, or until the vegetables are tender.

Pass them through a sieve, or beat to a puree with a
wooden spoon. Blend 1½ dessertspoons of flour to a
smooth cream with a little cold milk, then add some of
the hot stock to it. Return all to the saucepan, stirring,
bring to the boil, and simmer for at least 10 minutes. Add
the remainder of the milk, reheat, season, and serve the
hot soup with home-made rusks of wheatmeal bread
(see p. 111, BREAD AND BAKING).

ARTICHOKES AND POTATOES IN CAPER SAUCE

1 lb. mixed cooked artichokes and potatoes.	capers or pickled nasturtium seeds and 1 teaspoon
½ pint white sauce to which about 2 teaspoons chopped	vinegar have been added. Browned breadcrumbs.

A few shavings of cooking fat.

Dice the cooked artichokes and potatoes into neat cubes, placing them in a fireproof dish. Prepare the sauce, using part artichoke stock and part milk (see p. 115).

Pour the hot well-seasoned sauce over the vegetables, sprinkle with browned crumbs, dot here and there with cooking fat, and heat through in a moderately hot oven, or under a well-heated grill, until crisp-crusted and golden. Serve hot.

ARTICHOKE CHIPS

Another appetising way to cook this vegetable is to cut across the artichoke to make thinnish slices. These can be fried, like potato chips, in a little fat, then drained, salted, and seasoned with pepper, and perhaps a sprinkling of finely " powdered " cheese, if it can be spared. (The dry, next-to-the-rind pieces of hard cheese grate down excellently for this.)

ARTICHOKE CRISPS

Peel the artichokes and slice very thinly. Soak in well-salted water for about half an hour. Dry on a wire cake tray in a very slow oven until quite crisp (about 3 hours). Store in air-tight tins. These crisps are as delicious as potato crisps and have a pleasant flavour.

ASPARAGUS

Unless home-grown, asparagus is a luxury vegetable.

If buying asparagus, see that the stalks are fresh, the heads crisp and the cut ends of the stalk clear-coloured. If they are to be kept fresh for a few hours, place the stems in a jug of cold water.

To Cook.—Scrape the stem lightly with a knife, then wash in cold water. Trim the stalks to one length, and tie into conveniently-sized bundles.

Cook gently in boiling salted water, or steam in a small amount of water, with the heads emerging, until the green part of the stem is quite tender. Drain on a fish slice.

and lay the bundles on slices of toast. Snip the strings and dress the tips with as much melted fat—margarine for preference—as can be spared.

BROAD BEANS

As a pod vegetable, broad beans are valuable food. They contain vitamins A, C, and B 1, and good vegetable protein. Freshly picked, when young, they are really delicious.

Steamed, or boiled in a little salted water, they soon become tender, but be sure to leave on the outer skins of the seeds. Many people make the mistake of peeling away this covering skin, which deprives the dish of much flavour and food value.

Serve cooked broad beans with a little melted fat and a sprinkling of fresh chopped parsley. When a little older, they taste good in a parsley sauce, or with piquant flavouring.

Young broad beans are also good eaten raw in a salad.

BROAD BEANS (make two meals)

When young, broad beans can be used in two ways. The pods are very tender and delicious when sliced like runner beans, simmered in salted water and dressed in exactly the same way. They are also good served in parsley sauce.

Shell the beans in the usual way and cook for the first meal. Cut the pods into strips or diagonal slices, and cook them too. When cold, the sliced pods are good dressed in mayonnaise or French dressing in salad.

BROAD BEANS (cooked in their pods)

1 lb. very young beans.	1 dessertspoon of finely chopped parsley.
1 oz. margarine or bacon dripping.	1 gill bean liquor.
1 oz. flour.	1 gill milk.

Seasoning of salt and pepper.

Trim the end from the pods and cut the beans into inch lengths. Cook in boiling salted water until tender, then drain.

Make a parsley sauce with the bean stock, fat and flour, adding the milk after the sauce has fully cooked. Shake in the chopped parsley, season with salt and pepper, and mix in the cooked beans last of all. Heat through and serve.

BROAD BEAN PUREE

When beans are a little older, they can be sieved and
"creamed" to make them more attractive for table.
Take a quart measure of shelled beans and steam or boil
them in the usual way till tender.

Drain them, then rub them through a sieve. Take the
remaining liquor and make up to the required quantity
of liquid with milk, for a white sauce. Use an ounce of
bacon dripping or margarine and an ounce of flour for
each gill and a half of stock (for method, see p. 115), and
use the sauce, after boiling and seasoning, to bring the
puree to a creamy consistency.

For BROAD BEAN SALAD see p. 61, SALADS.

BROAD BEANS IN PIQUANT SAUCE

Boil the prepared beans until tender, then prepare a
sauce with 1 oz. margarine or cooking fat, 1 level tablespoon flour, and $\frac{1}{4}$ pint of stock from the beans.

Melt the fat, stir in the flour smoothly and allow them
to cook together slowly. Gradually add the gill of stock,
stirring until fully thickened. When returned to the boil
for three minutes, season well, and add 1 tablespoon of
vinegar, and $\frac{1}{2}$ teaspoon of chopped capers.

Heat the beans in this sauce, then serve while very hot.

BROAD BEANS FOR WINTER USE

Broad beans which have been allowed to mature in
their pods may be stored for winter use. Make sure they
are quite dry before packing in airtight tins. Soak and
cook like haricots.

FRENCH BEANS (or Runner Beans)

When young these vegetables can be cooked whole,
with tops and tails removed. When older, a stringy vein
develops down the ribs of the pod, which must be removed
before cooking for full enjoyment.

Trim away the "strings," then slice the bean lengthways, or break with the fingers into 2-inch lengths (this
saves time), and steam or boil the vegetable until tender
in a small quantity of boiling salted water. When tender
and young allow them to "steam" by using very little
water, and adding, if possible, a very little fat which they
can absorb during the cooking. This makes them glisten

well and improves their flavour. The actual cooking time varies with the age and size of the beans.

When beans are home-grown and can be gathered near the time of cooking, their full flavour and goodness can be enjoyed ; for households purchasing from local markets, it is wise to select beans as crisp as possible.

When runner beans are too old for table, let them mature on the plants and then dry the beans (not the pods) for winter use.

For FRENCH AND RUNNER BEANS IN SALADS, see p. 61, SALADS.

BEETROOT

Here is a favourite vegetable that can play a number of different roles. The sugar it contains makes it acceptable for salads, whether cooked or raw, or it can be baked or fried to develop a still more attractive flavour.

In preparing the vegetable, it is important to avoid breaking the skin, or the rich red colour " bleeds " away in the cooking.

Beet tops can be used as a vegetable too, and are as delicious as spinach if steamed or boiled in a very little water.

To cook the beets, wash them well in cold water, then boil steadily in salted water for 2 hours or more with the lid on the pan, until they feel tender. Press with the back of a wooden spoon to test, but do not prod with a fork, or the juices will escape. Drain them, and peel away the skin quickly.

BAKED BEETROOTS

When the oven is on, try baking the beetroots, without fat or water, as you would potatoes, or wrap them in a margarine paper and bake as before. They will take about 2 hours, if medium-sized.

To serve hot.—Cut quickly into quarters, and serve in a hot vegetable dish with a little melted fat and a sprinkling of chopped parsley. Or, pour a little thin white sauce over them.

To serve cold in salad, first slice the cooked beetroot thinly or cut into dice, and dress with vinaigrette (two parts salad oil to one of vinegar with seasonings). Arrange neatly in a salad dish, with a ring of chopped celery round, and a topping of either grated horseradish or chopped apple.

HOT BEETROOTS WITH HORSERADISH SAUCE

Small young beetroots.	Salt.
1 oz. flour.	1 tablespoon horseradish cream
1 oz. fat.	or 1 dessertspoon grated
½ pint milk, or vegetable stock	horseradish.
and milk mixed.	1 tablespoon vinegar.

Boil or bake the beetroots in the usual way. Drain, peel, and place them in a hot dish, quartered if large. Prepare a coating sauce with the flour, fat and milk (see p. 115), season with salt, and add the horseradish and vinegar.

Pour over the beetroot and serve very hot.

BEETROOT JELLY

1 small cooked beetroot.	1 small teacup vinegar.
1 pint tablet jelly (vanilla or	¼ teaspoon salt.
red-currant).	½ teaspoon pepper.

¾ pint water.

Cut up the jelly and dissolve in ½ pint of hot water, then make up to ¾ pint in all, with extra cold water. Dice the beetroot quite finely and arrange it in a pint mould, or several smaller sized ones, seasoning with the pepper and salt.

Add the vinegar to the jelly when quite cold, and while still liquid pour into the moulds to set.

Made in smaller quantities with left-over cooked beetroot; this is attractive if served with salad for a simple lunch or supper meal, adding hard-boiled egg to make it more substantial.

CABBAGE

Remember the importance of vitamins when choosing cooking methods, and try to serve cabbage raw sometimes, to save the Vitamin C.

To cook cabbage.—Slice finely and place in a saucepan with a sprinkling of salt and a teacupful of boiling water. Cover, and boil steadily for about 15 minutes. Shake the pan several times during cooking.

If it can be spared, add a little margarine or dripping to the water. Strain off any liquid left in the saucepan and use it for gravy or soup. Serve the cabbage piping hot.

All sorts of additions can be made with cabbage cooked in this way, to vary the flavour. A few bacon rinds chopped small, a few teaspoons of vinegar, and a shake of caraway seeds, or a sprinkling of nutmeg, and your cabbage becomes a continental dish. Always cook steadily with the lid on the pan and sprinkle with a little' pepper just before serving.

STUFFED CABBAGE

1 cabbage.
Salt and pepper.
Chopped parsley.
8 oz. browned wheatmeal breadcrumbs.

A little minced onion or chopped spring onion.
¼ lb. cooked liver, mince, or sausage meat.

Remove the outside leaves, clean and soak the cabbage whole in salted water. Par-boil in boiling salted water for about 5 minutes. Hollow out the cabbage by removing the centre leaves with a sharp knife and fill with the following stuffing.

Mix the chopped liver or meat with the breadcrumbs, add seasonings of pepper and salt, a little chopped parsley and minced onion, then mix to a binding consistency with vegetable boilings.

Pack the stuffing firmly in the cavity, tie the head securely with string, and steam until perfectly tender (about 20 to 25 minutes). (Serves 4.)

The cabbage leaves removed from the centres are useful for salads. Or mixed with mashed potato for vegetable pancakes or breakfast cakes.

CREAMED CABBAGE

1 medium-sized white-hearted cabbage.
Salt and pepper.
1 oz. dripping or margarine.
½ pint milk and water.

Wash the cabbage thoroughly in cold water to which a little salt has been added, and shred it. Heat ½ pint of milk, then melt an ounce of dripping in it. Add the shredded cabbage and cook steadily until tender, about 15 minutes.

Season with salt and pepper, and serve very hot with the liquid poured round it. This dish is particularly tasty if served with a spoonful of frizzled chopped bacon or a little grated cheese for topping. (Serves 4.)

If the inner section of the cabbage is cooked this way, reserve the *outer leaves* for the following recipe.

STUFFED CABBAGE LEAVES

Choose the outer green leaves from a tender cabbage, and cook them for a few minutes to make them pliable for rolling.

Make up a simple forcemeat, using either cooked minced meat or cooked sausage-meat, the same amount of breadcrumbs or mashed potato, a suspicion of chopped onion, a liberal sprinkle of chopped parsley and pepper and salt to taste. Bind with a little stock or gravy, and place a spoonful on each leaf.

Roll up and secure with thread, placing them to cook in a casserole in simmering stock to a depth to some half-way up the rolls. Cook until the leaves are tender— about 20 minutes or so—basting from time to time.

Serve on mashed potato, with well-seasoned brown gravy.

CABBAGE PLATE

I cabbage.	I oz. dripping or cooking fat.
Level dessertspoon curry powder.	I lb. potatoes.
	I teaspoon salt.

Shred the cabbage, including the stump, which can be cut into small dice after removing the fibrous outer part. Wash the cabbage in salted water then drain in a colander. Scrub the potatoes thoroughly, but do not remove the peel. They can then be cut into dice, of about ½ inch square.

Melt the fat in a deep frying pan, or suitable saucepan, and when quite hot add the vegetables. Sprinkle in the teaspoon of salt and curry powder, then stir thoroughly over moderate heat, cover and cook for a few minutes.

Remove the lid, and continue to cook for about 15 minutes, stirring continuously, but do not add any liquid.

When the vegetables become brown and are quite tender remove and serve fresh and hot. Eaten with wheatmeal bread, this makes a satisfying and appetising meal. It is also a good sandwich filling for a carried lunch. (Serves 4.)

RED CABBAGE CASSEROLE

I small red cabbage.	I dessertspoon flour.
½ lb. apples.	Piece of bay leaf.
A small onion, or a little minced spring onion.	½ pint water, or stock.
	I oz. dripping.
Salt and pepper. Dessertspoon of vinegar (if liked).	

Wash and halve the cabbage, remove the centre tough stalk, and shred the leaves into thin slices.

Chop the onion finely, and peel, core and quarter the apples. Place cabbage, onion and apples into the melted dripping in a casserole and sauté for a few minutes. Then add a pinch of salt and the measured water, and simmer gently until the cabbage is tender, adding vinegar if liked.

This vegetable is excellent served with sausages, or to make it a meal in itself, add a little chopped bacon just before the cabbage is to be served. (Serves 4).

CAULIFLOWER

Here is a valuable winter vegetable, which can be eaten either raw or cooked. The flower head can be grated raw for salads, while the green stem is excellent as a separate green vegetable serving. Always ask the greengrocer for the leaves of the cauliflower so that they can be cooked and served with the vegetable, or reserved for another dish.

The vitamin value of the vegetable is retained better if the cauliflower is separated into sprigs and cooked for a shorter time. A few of these can then be set aside for a cold salad, with a final dressing of vinaigrette.

Prepare the vegetable by trimming the stalk, cutting away, but reserving the outer leaves, and washing all in plenty of cold water. Soak the head for 20 minutes in warm salted water to draw away the insects, divide into springs, then rinse and steam or boil in a very little salted water until tender.

After draining the sprigs, dip in browned breadcrumbs, or serve with a coating of plain, well-seasoned white sauce. Here are a few other ways of dealing with cauliflower for vegetable meals.

CURRIED CAULIFLOWER

1 cauliflower.	A little minced onion, if possible.
A few sultanas, if possible.	1 dessertspoon curry powder.
1 apple.	1 oz. flour.

Cook the cauliflower as described above, then drain and save the stock. Measure ½ pint of cauliflower stock into a saucepan, add the prepared and sliced apple and the sultanas, and cook until soft.

Mix one dessertspoon of curry powder with an ounce of flour, then moisten with a little stock to a smooth cream. Add to the saucepan and stir until the mixture thickens, adding sufficient stock to bring to a pouring consistency. Then add the cauliflower sprigs to heat through, seasoning if necessary.

A little home-made jam or sweet pickle is an improvement with curry sauce, if you have some handy.

Serve the curry in the centre of a round dish, with a ring of mashed potato round it.

BAKED CAULIFLOWER

2 small cauliflowers.	1 teaspoon of vegetable extract
2 tablespoons breadcrumbs	(yeast product) if liked.
(wheatmeal).	1 oz. dripping or cooking fat.
1 gill milk.	1½ oz. flour.

Cook the cauliflowers as described on page 19. Then drain carefully and reserve the liquid, using it for the sauce, in part measure with milk.

Grease a fireproof dish and arrange the cauliflower sprigs in it, keeping them hot while making the white sauce. For this use 1½ oz. flour, 1 oz. fat and 1 gill milk. When boiled and smooth, add 2 gills of cauliflower stock in which the extract has been dissolved. Season well.

Pour the sauce over the cooked cauliflower, sprinkle with an even coating of browned breadcrumbs, and cook in a moderate oven till crisp. For a quick meal, brown beneath a heated grill until well coloured, and serve very hot.

CARROTS

The carrot is one of the most valuable of all root vegetables. It is a rich source of Carotene, which is converted into Vitamin A, and strengthens our resistance to infection.

Carrots also contain sugar, which is useful for war-time diet. Most children like raw carrots and should be allowed to eat them freely.

Two tablespoons of grated raw carrot daily is a good rule for both children and adults. This can be served in a salad, or taken in a wheatmeal bread sandwich. Here are some sandwich fillings to try.

(See page 60, SALADS).

SANDWICH FILLINGS.

RAW.

1. Add two parts of grated raw carrot to one part of finely shredded white heart of cabbage, and bind with finely chopped sweet pickle. Season to taste.

2. *For children*—use the filling without pickle, and spread the slice with a little dripping, or margarine mixed with a little vegetable extract. This increases the nourishment and adds to the vitamin value.

COOKED.

3. Prepare and cut the carrot into small cubes, cooking

them in well-blended curry sauce. When perfectly tender and yielding to the knife, use as sandwich filling.

4. Chopped cooked carrot, mixed with cooked peas and a little mayonnaise or salad dressing, makes a good filling or salad.

UNCOOKED CARROT PUDDING

2 medium-sized carrots.	1 tablespoon browned crumbs.
2 tablespoons of ground nuts (in season).	1 tablespoon fresh milk.
½ gill warm water, in which is dissolved 1 dessertspoon honey.	1 teaspoon " top milk."
	1 teaspoon fruit juice (in season).
	1 tablespoon rolled oats or toasted oatmeal.

Wash, scrape, and grate the carrots. Melt the honey in the warm water. Use the liquid to mix the milled nuts, grated carrot, oatmeal and crumbs.

Sharpen with the fruit juice, then add the milk and allow the sweet to stand a short time before serving it in small individual dishes. Use a little " top milk " as a substitute for cream.

CARROT CROQUETTES

6 good-sized carrots.	1 oz. flour.
1 oz. cooking fat or dripping.	Coarse oatmeal for coating.
A little fat for frying.	¼ teaspoon vegetable extract (if liked).
1 gill milk and carrot boilings.	

Slice the carrots and cook in a very little water until tender (see page 11). Drain well, saving the liquid, and mash with a fork until pureed. Season well with salt, add a grate of nutmeg and shake of pepper.

Make a thick sauce with the flour, liquid and fat (see page 115), and work the puree and vegetable extract into it. Set aside to cool.

When cold, shape into croquettes. Roll in coarse oatmeal that has been previously toasted a little in the oven or under the grill. Fry in a little fat, turning to colour the cakes evenly. Drain and serve hot with good gravy. Or bake in the oven.

PARSLEY CARROTS

1½ lb. carrots.	Salt, pepper.
Teacup of stock or water, or sufficient to cover.	Small piece of dripping or margarine.
3 dessertspoons chopped parsley.	

Scrub the carrots and cut them into slices, about ¼ inch in thickness. Heat the fat in the pan and sauté the carrots, frying them without browning for about 10 minutes, shaking occasionally. Add 1 gill of stock or water, bringing the level to just cover.

Cook gently until the carrots are tender—about 25-35 minutes. Drain the carrots, reduce the liquid a little by boiling, and sprinkle the chopped parsley (or the chopped feathery carrot tops) over the dish. Pour the reduced seasoned stock over the vegetable and serve at once.

SAVOURY CARROT CASSEROLE

Young carrots and green peas— sufficient to fill a casserole, using twice as much carrots as peas.	2 tablespoons of milk. Parsley sauce to cover. A little minced onion, or rings of spring onion.
2 small sprigs of mint.	Salt, pepper.

Prepare enough carrots and green peas to fill the selected casserole, using twice as much carrot as peas.

Scrape and dice the carrots, place them in the casserole, just cover with salted water, bring them to the boil and simmer for five minutes. Then add the peas, the chopped mint, minced onion, a pinch of salt, and the milk. Cover with a close-fitting lid and cook gently in the oven until the carrots are perfectly tender.

Prepare a plain parsley sauce (see p. 115), using ½ pint of liquid from the casserole, 1 oz. flour and ½ oz. margarine or dripping, and season well. Add 2 dessertspoons of finely chopped parsley just before serving. Pour this over the vegetables, replace the lid, and serve very hot.

CARROT ROLL

2 large carrots.	1 dessertspoon fine oatmeal.
Cold cooked mashed potato.	1 teaspoon vegetable extract.

Grate the scrubbed carrots on a suet grater and cook for 10 minutes in a very little water. Season well and add 1 teaspoon of vegetable extract and 1 dessertspoon of toasted fine oatmeal.

Boil five minutes, stirring, to thicken, then set to cool. At this stage the mixture should be quite stiff.

Have ready some cold mashed potatoes, dust the pastry board and pin with flour, and roll out to an oblong shape. Place the carrot filling in the centre, then fold over and shape to a roll. Dot with a few shavings of fat and bake till nicely browned in a moderately hot oven. Serve with well-seasoned brown gravy.

CARROTS AND SPROUTS

Choose equal quantities of sprouts and carrots by

weight, prepare them in the usual way, slicing both to convenient size.

Steam together until tender (about 15 minutes), sprinkling them with a little salt in the steamer.

Alternatively—cook in a very little water in a saucepan, starting the carrots a little ahead of the green sprouts to enable them to finish cooking together. Use the liquor, with added vegetable extract, as sauce. Dress in a little dripping or cooking fat just before serving, adding a small shake of pepper.

CARROT BEEHIVE

About 1½ lb. carrots. | Salt and pepper.
¾ lb. potato suet crust. | Gravy powder.

Wash and scrape the carrots. Make 1 lb. potato suet crust (see p. 59). Line a greased pudding bowl with it, then put in a layer of grated raw carrot (about 1 inch deep). Sprinkle with salt, pepper and gravy powder, and cover with a very thin circle of the crust, cut to fit. Repeat the layers of carrot and crust until the basin is full, ending with crust. Cover with margarine paper and steam for 2½-3 hours. Serve with brown gravy.

CURRIED CARROTS AND CELERY

2 lb. carrots. | Dash of vinegar.
¼ head celery. | 1 tablespoon home made jam.
1 oz. dripping. | 2 teaspoons curry powder.
¾ pint vegetable boilings or water. | 1 apple, peeled and sliced.
½ oz. flour. | A little minced onion, or spring onion.

Scrape and slice the carrots. Prepare the celery and chop fairly fine. Melt the dripping in the pan, put in the apple, minced onion and celery, and sauté for a few minutes without browning. Add the curry powder and flour and fry lightly, stirring well.

Next add the stock or water, vinegar, etc., and stir well until thickened, before adding the carrots and jam. Cover, and simmer for 20 minutes to half an hour.

Serve with a border of creamily mashed potatoes.

CARROT SPREAD (see PACKED MEALS, p. 121).

CARROT PUDDING (see Peace and War Pudding, p. 59, POTATOES).

CELERY

At a time when salad vegetables are less plentiful comes celery—a useful Vitamin C vegetable. When lettuce is unobtainable, and you want a change from grated cabbage, try young celery leaves in your winter salads. Fresh or dried, they also make good flavouring for casserole and stews.

The best way to serve celery raw is to separate the cleaned stalks, selecting the centre crisp stems for salads, and the " heart " for table use. The outer sections are good braised, served as a vegetable accompaniment, or included in a casserole.

Prepare celery by washing well in a bowl of cold water, then splitting the head and separating the stalks for similar treatment. Leave to crisp or curl in ice-cold water, the shorter stems in a jug or deep basin. Cut celery stalks, trimmed and left in cold water, will curl attractively for serving in a celery vase, or chopped in the salad. Fine curled shreds look most inviting arranged with other, more colourful, vegetables.

CREAMED CELERY

1 good head of celery.	¾ pint milk and water.
A few browned breadcrumbs.	¾ oz. fat.
Pepper and salt.	¾ oz. flour.

Wash the celery, trim it into lengths, dice and place in a casserole or deep pie dish. Cover with the milk and water, add salt, and simmer until tender.

Drain, saving the liquid for the sauce.

Prepare the sauce as in recipe, p. 115. Simmer for three minutes, then add a generous sprinkling of pepper and salt (if necessary) before replacing the cooked celery. Return to the casserole, sprinkle with browned breadcrumbs, heat through and serve hot.

FRIED CELERY

1 head of celery	A little flour and water for a
A little fat for frying.	thin batter.

Wheatmeal breadcrumbs.

Prepare the celery and trim into short lengths. Simmer these in salted water until tender, then drain, saving the liquid for soup. Make a thin frying batter of flour and water, dip each portion into this, drain, roll in crumbs and fry until lightly browned. Three to four minutes' frying should be sufficient, turning the pieces until they colour and crisp.

Serve with a light shaking of vinegar.

CUCUMBER

Not only is cucumber useful as a sandwich filling, or as raw vegetable in salads, but it is excellent steamed or fried. Don't peel the cucumber ; the outside skin makes it more digestible.

Made into small " cups "—by trimming the cucumber into small lengths and scooping out one end—the vegetable can be stuffed, or par-cooked, and used to hold small quantities of sauce-bound foods—meat or fish.

A very attractive effect is obtained by stripping off the skin at regular intervals to a width of $\frac{1}{8}$ inch, so that the cups appear to be striped. If time is short, it is best to keep the skin on the vegetable entirely, rather than remove it and cause waste by careless cutting. When stuffed, steam for about 30 minutes.

STEWED CUCUMBER

Slice the cucumber thickly and cook for about 10 minutes in boiling salted water. Drain, and thicken the liquid with a little flour to make a sauce, as described on p. 115. Return the cucumber to the sauce, heat up and serve as a green vegetable.

ROASTED CUCUMBER

Cut a medium-sized cucumber into 2-inch lengths and boil for 4 to 5 minutes in a little salted water. Roll in breadcrumbs, put in a baking tin with a little fat and bake until golden brown (about 5 mins.).

CUCUMBER SAUCE, see p. 115, SAUCES.

LEEKS

(See also p. 108, SOUP.)

To prepare leeks—trim off the roots, the outer tops and the sheath coverings. Split them down the centre and wash very thoroughly, as they hold grit between the folds. Allow them to soak for 20 minutes to half an hour in cold salted water, to ensure they are clear. Then drain, and cook until tender in a very little boiling salted water, from 20-30 minutes according to size.

Drain them well, and serve with a simple white sauce.

LEEK PUDDING
POTATO SUET CRUST PASTRY

8 oz. flour (self-raising)	*Filling*—2-3 large leeks, or six
2 oz. finely chopped suet.	small ones.
2 oz. grated raw potato.	Pepper and salt.

Trim the leeks, cut in four lengthwise, wash thoroughly and slice finely into 1-inch lengths.

Make up the pastry, and line a pudding basin with two-thirds of it, leaving the remaining piece to form a lid, rolling it to a round the exact size.

Fill up the basin with the cut leeks, seasoning at each layer. Lay the lid in position, damp the edges, and seal together. Cover with a greased paper, place in the steamer and cook for about 2 hours. Serve with a good brown gravy.

Another method.—Form the pastry into an oval about ¼ inch thick. Spread the chopped leeks over the pastry and sprinkle with seasoning. Dampen the edges of the pastry and roll up firmly. Wrap tightly in a margarine paper, and steam for an hour and a half.

LETTUCE

Lettuce is at its most valuable when served raw (see p. 60, SALADS). These recipes for cooked lettuce may come in useful when you want to vary the vegetable course.

LETTUCE AS A GREEN VEGETABLE

Wash and quarter the lettuces, and cook in a very little salted water until tender (about 10 minutes). Drain well, saving the liquid for soup.

LETTUCE AND SPINACH

Lettuce and spinach, cooked together, half and half make a pleasant change.

BRAISED LETTUCE WITH PEAS

4 small lettuce.	½ gill stock.
½ gill shelled peas.	1 teaspoon of chopped parsley.
Bouquet of herbs (tied in muslin).	1½-2 oz. dripping or cooking fat.
	Salt, pepper.
2-3 spring onions chopped.	

Wash and prepare the lettuces, breaking up the large leaves, then place them in a saucepan in which the dripping has been melted and heated. Allow to sauté in the fat with the chopped onion for a few minutes, then add the stock, seasoning of salt and a little pepper, with the shelled peas.

Cover, allow the stock to come to the boil, and continue the cooking for about half an hour, with the pan tightly covered.

Just before the dish is to be served, add a sprinkling of freshly chopped parsley.

STUFFED LETTUCE

2-3 good-sized lettuces (Cos).	½ pint stock or vegetable boil-
1 oz. margarine.	ings, milk and water, etc.
¾ oz. flour.	Seasoning.

Wash the lettuces, and cook gently in the liquid for 5 minutes. Lift them out, halve lengthwise, and remove some of the hearts.

Fill the cavities with the stuffing below, tie the halves together with thread, and replace in the stewpan or casserole to complete the cooking. When tender, thicken the liquid with a binding of fat and flour, loosened by the hot stock, and boil for three minutes. Serve round the dish with the lettuces.

STUFFING.—3 oz. medium oatmeal; 1 heaped tea-spoon chopped parsley; salt; pepper; 1 dessertspoon melted dripping; 2 oz. breadcrumbs; 1 heaped teaspoon minced onion; 1 good teaspoon vegetable extract; pinch of mace.

Toast the oatmeal beforehand, under the grill or in a cooling oven, till crisp and nutty. Dissolve the vegetable extract in ½ pint of boiling water, then sprinkle in the oatmeal and cook, stirring, till thick and allowing to simmer for half an hour.

Then mix in with the other ingredients, binding with a little melted dripping. Season well, and use to stuff the hollowed lettuce. (Any lettuce hearts removed from the centre are useful additions to soup or vegetable casseroles.)

STUFFED MARROW

Cut a medium-sized marrow in two lengthways and scoop out the seeds. Fill with stuffing made of a breakfast-cupful of wheatmeal breadcrumbs (use any left-over pieces of bread for this), 2 tablespoonfuls minced fat bacon, 2 spring onions chopped, sprinkling of mixed herbs, pepper and salt, bound with a little milk.

Put the halves together, tie round with tape or string, put in a baking tin with about 1 oz. dripping and bake until tender (about 1 hour) basting frequently.

MARROW AU GRATIN

1 medium-sized marrow.	Mushroom sauce—made from
1-2 spoonfuls milk.	2 oz. chopped mushroom
1 oz. fat bacon (rasher).	stalks, 1½ gills stock or
Toasted oatmeal.	water, ¾ oz. flour.

Peel the marrow, remove the seeds and cut it into small pieces. Place in a saucepan with just enough water to prevent it catching, add a pinch of salt, and " steam " until all the water has evaporated.

Next add the chopped fat bacon and sauté a short time for the flavour to be absorbed, then season well, and sprinkle with a little toasted oatmeal.

Make the mushroom sauce, then turn the marrow and chopped bacon mixture into a greased dish, pour on the sauce, and sprinkle with toasted oatmeal to form a crisp cap. Brown off quickly in the oven (or under a grill) and serve hot.

MUSHROOMS

When they are in season, field or downland mushrooms make delightful flavouring for vegetable dishes, as well as attractive stuffings to make meat meals go further.

Although cultivated mushrooms are available throughout the year, the price is rather too high for most people in war-time. Often, however, it is possible to buy the trimmed stalks from greengrocers at a few pence the pound, and these are worth consideration for their flavour alone, especially in casseroles, soups, and savoury toasts.

For whole mushrooms, the simplest ways of cooking are best. Grill them if you can. Wash them first, then peel the caps, cut off the stalks (which go into hotpot stew, or, chopped fine, into soups or sauces) and dry lightly.

Brush the caps and underside with melted margarine or oil, sprinkle with salt, and lay on the grid. Turn with a couple of spoons or tongs during cooking, but be careful not to leave them too long under the strong heat. Serve on squares of toast as a savoury snack or supper serving.

Mushrooms are also good fried in a very little fat, or stewed gently with a little stock or milk and water. Remember to season them well, and thicken the stock with a little blended flour just before serving.

NETTLES

Used instead of spinach, nettles are excellent food. Rich in the two vitamins A and C, the young leaves are especially good. They should be gathered early in spring.

Wash them well, and allow a good panful, as you would for spinach. Cook in their own juices, with a very little water.

When young and tender, they will take about ten

minutes, after which they can be drained, the water put aside for soup, and the vegetable chopped finely and reheated in a little fat if you can spare it. Margarine is best for flavour, when butter cannot be spared. Add seasoning, a grate of nutmeg, heat through, and serve.

NETTLE CHAMP

Nettles are an excellent ingredient for the Irish recipe with potatoes. See page 53, POTATOES, for the foundation method.

The Irish way of eating " champ " is for each person to make a hole in the centre of his helping in which a pat of margarine is gradually melted by the heat of the potato. As he eats from the outer rim of the helping, he dips each spoonful into the melted fat.

ONIONS

When onions are plentiful, remember that they are delicious parboiled and stuffed or made into an oven-bake.

BRAISED ONIONS

4-6 onions. | 1 oz. dripping. | Seasoning.

Prepare the onions, peeling them and splitting into halves or quarters. Melt the dripping in a fireproof dish, by placing it in the oven, then arrange the onions in it, seasoning well.

Pour in about a teacupful of water. Simmer the onions, basting every few minutes, until they have become a good colour, then allow to simmer for a further half-hour to forty minutes, according to the size and type of onion.

STUFFED ONIONS

4 large sized onions.	For the Filling—
Salt and pepper.	4 oz. browned breadcrumbs.
	2 oz. minced meat.
	Salt and pepper.

Peel the onions and simmer in a little salted water until tender. Drain (saving the water) and scoop out the centres. Chop the centres and mix with the stuffing ingredients, moistening with a little onion water if necessary. Fill the onions with the mixture and bake them on a lightly greased baking tin until brown on top. A few browned breadcrumbs sprinkled over the top helps to crisp them.

BAKED ONIONS

If you have a cottage kitchener, try baking onions in their skins. They take rather a long time, about 2 hours in a moderate oven, but they have a splendid flavour and are particularly comforting in cold weather.

To bake onions more quickly, first steam for about ten minutes then place in the oven for 1 hour.

ONION SKINS

Dry all the outside onion skins in a moderate oven until crisp enough to crumble. Store in an airtight tin and use for flavouring soups and stews.

PARSNIPS

Like carrot, parsnip is a root with good sugar content. For this reason it is delicious when cooked in a very little fat—either baked beneath the meat or fried.

A good way to cook parsnips is to boil them whole (30 to 40 minutes), after careful washing, keeping on the skins. These can then be rubbed off quite easily when the vegetable is tender.

A little finely shredded raw parsnip adds a new and delicious flavour to a mixed vegetable salad. Cooked parsnip, cut into neat dice, can also be used in salads.

STUFFED PARSNIPS

Parboil or steam the parsnips, divide into two lengthwise and remove the centre cores. Fill with forcemeat made of breadcrumbs seasoned with mixed herbs, salt and pepper, and bound with a little milk. Put the halves together again and secure with string. Dot with dripping and bake in a moderate oven until golden brown, basting frequently.

PARSNIP CROQUETTES

1 lb. (cold) cooked parsnips.	1 heaped teaspoon vegetable extract.
1 gill vegetable stock or milk.	
1 oz. flour.	1 oz. dripping or cooking fat.

Salt, pepper.

Sieve, or mash the parsnips with a fork, till creamy. Then make a thick sauce with the fat, flour, and stock (in which the vegetable extract has been dissolved, see p. 115). When cooked and thick, work in a few breadcrumbs if liked.

Add the parsnips, and season to taste. Then set aside to firm on a plate. Divide into 10-12 pieces, and form into croquettes.

Roll in browned breadcrumbs, or dip in a flour and water batter (mixed very thinly) and coat in crumbs, patting them on well. Fry in a hot fat till golden brown on both sides. Alternatively—the cakes could be baked.

PARSNIP PIE

2-3 cooked parsnips.
½ pint coating sauce—(see p. 115).
   using half parsnip water, half milk.

1 tablespoon minced onion.
Finely chopped parsley.
Browned breadcrumbs, or toasted oatmeal, or mashed potatoes for the top.

Slice the cooked parsnip, or cut into neat dice, arranging a layer at the bottom of a deep fireproof dish. Pour in a layer of well-seasoned sauce, to which the chopped parsley and onion have been added. Sprinkle lightly with toasted oatmeal. Continue the layers till the dish is full.

Finally sprinkle well with oatmeal—or use a mashed potato crust—flake a little dripping over the top, and bake in a moderate oven from 20-30 minutes.

PEAS

Straight from the garden or allotment, pod vegetables are deliciously tender. Try to use them as soon as they are gathered, and shell them as near the time for cooking them as possible.

Never throw the pea pods away. When they are clear-skinned and fleshy, serve them as a second vegetable (see recipe on p. 32). If they are older, use them for soup. For recipe, see p. 107, SOUP.

The best way to cook garden peas is the continental way, with very little water and a little herb flavouring. Take a teacup of boiling salted water, a few shreds of onion, a sprig of mint and a small teaspoon of sugar.

Simmer the peas gently in an open pan until they are tender—about 10 to 15 minutes for young ones is sufficient. When the season advances, the older ones may take up to 25 or 30 minutes to become tender.

Another excellent way to cook young peas is to steam them with a few sprigs of mint and a sprinkling of salt. They will cook in about 15 minutes and, this way, are full of flavour.

PEAS AND CARROTS

1 lb. shelled peas.	Few leaves of mint.
Small piece of dripping or margarine.	3 medium-sized carrots.
	Salt, pepper.

Pinch of sugar, if possible.

Wash and scrub the carrots and cut into ¼-inch slices, or dice. Put them, with the peas, into a saucepan with just enough boiling water to cover. Add the mint, sugar and a little salt, cover and cook gently for about 20 minutes.

The cooking time depends on the age of the vegetables, and if the carrots are old they should be pre-cooked about 10 minutes before the peas are added to them.

When both are soft, strain the stock (reserving it for gravy or soup). Add the fat to the pan and shake the vegetables well as it melts, to gloss them. Add pepper to taste and serve hot.

PEA PODS

Use clear-skinned, fleshy pods for this recipe. Divide each pod into two. Hold one of the sections in your left hand, stalk end uppermost and inside towards you. Snap down about ½ inch of the pod at the stalk end towards you. Then, holding firmly, pull downward, stripping the inside skin from the outer. With a little practice, this is easy. Cook the fleshy *outsides* in a very little salted water until tender (about 10 minutes), drain and serve.

SPINACH

This vegetable is green, richly-flavoured and a good source of Vitamins A and C.

The important part in cooking spinach is the preparation of the leaves, which should be stripped from the centre stalks or " ribs "—which, incidentally are good chopped finely in salad. Wash the stripped leaves very thoroughly—five to six waters being necessary to extract all the grittiness that they collect.

Finally, drain them into a colander, and turn into a saucepan, with the water clinging to them, sprinkle with salt, and place them over low heat. Do not add any water. Sufficient moisture is extracted from the leaves to cook the vegetable.

About 10-15 minutes is sufficient time to allow, with an occasional shake to free the leaves in the pan. Drain and sieve at once or, if liked, chop lightly on a board, reheat, season, and serve. A light grating of nutmeg may be added.

BRAISED SPINACH

2 lb. spinach.	Small piece of turnip.
I large carrot.	Rinds from a rasher of bacon.
I onion, or a few spring onions.	I oz. dripping.
I gill (teacup) of stock.	Salt, pepper.

Wash the spinach very thoroughly in several waters. Remove the mid-ribs. Melt the dripping in the casserole. Add the carrot, turnip and onion, cut into small pieces. Then put in the bacon rinds.

Pour in the stock and add seasonings. Then add the spinach. Cover the top of the casserole with a piece of greased paper, replace the lid, and cook in a moderate oven till tender. Remove the spinach, chop it finely and strain over the stock from the braise.

The vegetables used for the braising " bed " are useful for soup afterwards, or, broken up with a fork, they could be served with the spinach.

SPINACH TOASTS

Allow for each person—

I tablespoon cooked spinach.	I dessertspoon milk.
I round of wheatmeal toast.	Tiny piece of fat.
½ egg.	Salt, pepper.

Drain the spinach well, season and chop it fairly finely. Melt the fat in a small saucepan. Beat up the egg with the milk, add a pinch of salt and shake of pepper. Stir in the spinach, then turn all into the saucepan for seven to eight minutes.

Cook over very low heat, stirring all the time. Pile on to hot toast, spread with a little mayonnaise if it can be spared, and serve at once.

SPINACH AU GRATIN

I lb. spinach.	¼ teaspoon fine nutmeg.
½ gill thick sauce (see p. 115)— flavoured with a grating of cheese.	A good knob of margarine or dripping (about ¼ oz.).
	Salt, pepper.
Breadcrumbs.	

Cook the spinach, then chop and dress with the fat. Add a quarter of a teaspoon of grated nutmeg, seasoning of salt and pepper, and bind with the sauce.

Place the spinach mixture in a greased fireproof dish, cover with breadcrumbs, or toasted oatmeal, mixed with a very little finely grated cheese.

Put a fleck or two of fat on the top, then bake in a

moderate oven for about 20 minutes to crisp the top and blend the flavours well.

SPINACH (with Rolled Oats)

2 lb. spinach.	2 oz. dripping or margarine.
2 oz. rolled oats.	½ gill (teacup) milk.
Seasoning to taste.	A grating of nutmeg.

Wash the spinach thoroughly, then cut up coarsely and put into boiling salted water (about ¾ pint). Sprinkle in the rolled oats to the quickly boiling water and spinach, boiling till the oats are cooked, by which time all the moisture should have been absorbed. (If it is necessary, add a little more boiling water.)

When the oats are done, stir in the milk, dripping, pepper and salt to taste, with nutmeg if liked. Keep over gentle heat, to keep hot without catching in the pan, for 8-10 minutes, then serve.

This makes a nourishing dish, which can be made even more substantial by adding to the spinach an equal quantity of mashed potato, with suitable seasoning. Or form the spinach, oatmeal and potato into a roll, binding it with a very little beaten egg. Form into a roll shape and bake in a moderate oven, cover with a margarine paper, which can be removed for the last part of the time, to colour the coating. This roll is useful served hot ; or cut cold for the centre of a vegetable " platter " with cooked vegetables or raw salads.

If preferred, shape the mixture into small cakes, toss on oatmeal and fry in shallow fat. When crisp and golden, drain and serve hot with piquant sauce (p. 116) or gravy.

SPROUTS

These vegetables are quick to cook and simple to serve. They are also excellent raw in salads.

Prepare them by cutting the " buds " level with the stalk, and cross-cutting the stalk to shorten the cooking time. Soak a short time in salted water, then rinse in cold water, drain and cook by boiling in a very little salted water or steaming until tender. About 15-20 minutes is the usual time for boiling sprouts. If they are to be steamed it is a good plan to shred them, when they will cook in 10 to 15 minutes.

When tender, drain well, dress with a small nut of margarine or dripping, shaking them to gloss well. Dust with black pepper, and serve on a very hot dish. Save the water in which they were boiled for soup.

BRUSSEL SPROUTS AND CELERY

I lb. cooked brussel sprouts.	I tablespoon flour.
Small piece of dripping or cooking fat.	½ head celery.
	½ pint milk or vegetable stock.

Prepare the celery and cut it into small pieces. Melt the fat and turn in the celery to cook in the saucepan slowly for two or three minutes.

Pour in the liquid, cover down, and cook by steady simmering until the celery is soft.

Blend the flour to a cream with a tablespoon of milk, and pour on a little of the celery stock. Return to the pan and stir well until the sauce thickens. Add the sprouts, season well, and reheat. Serve hot.

If preferred, the mixture can be turned into a fireproof dish, the top sprinkled with brown breadcrumbs and shavings of fat, and the whole crisped till brown in the oven, or under a heated grill.

SHROPSHIRE SWEDES

Equal amounts of swedes and potatoes.	Seasonings.
	Hot milk.
Chopped parsley.	

Take equal quantities of swedes and potatoes. Simmer both in salted water until soft, then drain and mash well. Add salt and pepper and a little hot milk.

A few shavings of margarine or dripping are a great improvement if they can be spared.

Reheat if necessary, and sprinkle lightly with finely chopped parsley.

SWEDES AND SPINACH

Mashed swedes, well seasoned and with a light topping of grated cheese, make an attractive serving ringed round with a border of chopped cooked spinach. Good seasoning, and a small grate of nutmeg, improves the spinach.

CASSEROLE OF SWEDES

I lb. swedes.	I oz. dripping or bacon fat.
I teaspoon flour.	I gill (teacup) water.
I teaspoon chopped parsley.	Seasoning.

Peel, wash and slice the swedes rather thinly, dry, and sprinkle with the flour, and fry quickly in the heated dripping till lightly browned.

Place in a casserole with the water, pepper and salt, cover and simmer gently till tender. Serve with the liquid in the pan, and sprinkle over with the chopped parsley.

"HOT" TURNIPS

1 lb. turnips.	1½ dessertspoons of flour.
1 oz. cooking fat or dripping.	1½ teaspoons made mustard.
½ pint turnip boilings.	Chopped spring onion.

Few drops vinegar.

Sauté the turnips in a little cooking fat, with a little chopped spring onion, or minced onion. Add half a pint of household stock and allow the turnips to simmer gently till tender.

Thicken the liquor with a dessertspoon and a half of blended flour, worked to a cream with cold water, and season with 1½ teaspoons of made mustard flavoured with a dash of vinegar, and the usual pepper and salt.

BAKED TURNIPS

Peel and slice some young turnips. Arrange them in layers in a fireproof dish, sprinkling each layer with salt, pepper, and a very little nutmeg. Pour over a cupful of milk, or milk and water, and sprinkle with browned crumbs on top. If available, include a spoonful of finely grated cheese with the crumbs.

Add a few shavings of margarine or dripping and bake in a moderate oven until the turnips are tender and the top brown and crisp.

TURNIP TOMMIES

Allow—

1 medium-sized turnip to each person.	1 sausage to each turnip, or the equivalent in meat croquette mixture.
Brown gravy.	

Wash the turnips, then pare evenly and score into four quarters without severing. Par-cook in boiling salted water for 10 minutes.

Drain well, then skin a sausage for each turnip, par-cook or fry, and force the meat between the quarters to hold firmly. Brush the sides with a very little dripping, roll or dust lightly in brown breadcrumbs, and place the tommies in a baking dish with a little water or stock and steam-bake until tender and crisp-topped.

Serve with good brown gravy and suitable green vegetable.

TURNIP PIE

4 young turnips.	1 teacup milk, or stock in which
½ teacup of wheatmeal bread-crumbs.	a little vegetable extract has been dissolved.

Small piece of fat.

Wash and cook the young turnips whole in boiling salted water until almost tender. Then drain and peel them while they are hot. Cut into slices and place them in a greased pie dish.

Sprinkle the layers with salt and pepper and chopped parsley. Pour over them the milk or vegetable stock in which a little vegetable extract has been dissolved—about a level teaspoon to the gill being sufficient.

Sprinkle well with breadcrumbs and a few shavings of fat, and put into a fairly hot oven until nicely browned— or under a heated grill if preferred.

TURNIP TOPS

The green tops of fresh young turnips are extremely good when served as a green vegetable, and they are particularly valuable for their protective qualities. Apart from their vitamin value, they contain essential mineral salts.

Turnip tops taste very much like spinach, and they are especially good when the vegetables are home grown and freshly pulled.

To prepare them—cut all the tops from the vegetables, and wash them very thoroughly to remove embedded grit. Shred and place in a pan with just enough water to prevent burning. Press them well down, and boil quickly for 10-15 minutes, then drain, saving any liquid for soup.

Season well with salt and pepper and serve very hot.

TOMATOES

Not only is the tomato an attractive vegetable, both in appearance and taste, but it offers some of the most important protective elements in diet. If you grow your own tomatoes you can be sure of eating them when they are fresh. They contain all four vitamins, A, B1, B2 and C.

Their juiciness makes them very easy and quick to cook, although they are certainly best taken raw in salad. Peel the tomatoes if they are sun-ripened, and slice them into the dish. Then spoon over them a simple vinegar dressing of tarragon or garlic vinegar, and a shake of pepper.

For a quickly cooked vegetable, grilled tomatoes are excellent. Shake a little pepper and salt on the halved tomatoes and dot with a few shavings of fat, before placing them under the heated grill. They take just four minutes.

STUFFED RAW TOMATOES

Halved medium-sized tomatoes. | Finely minced onion or chopped
Oil, vinegar. | spring onion.
Few scraps of fish or meat (finely | Chopped parsley, or sprigs
minced), cooked) if liked. | watercress.
Cooked rice.

To add to a green salad, or plate of vegetables, these are most attractive.

Prepare the cooked rice by mixing it with a very little minced onion, and dressing it with a little oil and vinegar. Season well.

If you have a few teaspoons of minced cooked meat or fish, these can be added as well.

Then halve the tomatoes, remove a very little of the pulp with a teaspoon, adding it to the rice. Then pile up the tomato cups with the prepared filling, and dust over with a little finely chopped parsley. A sprig or two of watercress looks attractive if the cups are to be arranged with salad.

HOT TOMATO SALAD

Slice the tomatoes, not too thinly, and spread each slice with a little mustard " butter." This is made by creaming a little margarine or suitable fat with made mustard to taste.

The mustard slices are then grilled or baked sufficiently long to blend the flavours.

This makes a good accompaniment for foods that need added flavour.

SPAGHETTI WITH PEAS AND TOMATOES

4 oz. spaghetti. | I dessertspoonful flour.
4 tomatoes. | Small knob of fat.
I cupful cooked peas. | Salt, Pepper.

Break up the spaghetti into small lengths and cook in boiling salted water until tender. Drain, and reserve the liquid.

Melt the fat in the saucepan, stir in the flour, and let it bubble and spread. Moisten with a cup of the spaghetti stock, and bring to the boil, stirring till thickened.

Add the tomatoes, cut into small pieces, and simmer with the pan covered for about 15-20 minutes. Return the cooked spaghetti to the pan, with the peas. Mix all together lightly, removing any loose portions of tomato skin.

Reheat, add a shake of cayenne pepper if liked, and serve with triangles of toast or with baked bread " rusks."

SAVOURY TOMATO PANCAKES

3 tomatoes.
2 oz. cooked minced liver.
1 gill stock, vegetable boilings or water.
Breadcrumbs.
Salt, pepper.

Pancake batter—using a basis of ½ egg (beaten), 2 oz. flour, 1 teacup milk ; or
Potato omelet—(" Floddie "), see page 47.

Make the batter in the usual way, working the flour smoothly with the egg and milk, beating it thoroughly while thick and creamy. Then add the rest of the milk and a pinch of salt.

If a potato omelet is being prepared, start this first of all, and while the mixture is cooking slowly and forming a crust, the filling can be made.

Skin and slice the tomatoes, and stew these in the stock until quite tender—about 10 minutes. Add the minced liver and enough breadcrumbs to bind together to a soft paste. Season well.

Melt a little cooking fat in the frying pan, and when it is smoking hot, pour in the batter and cook on both sides. Turn it out on to the hot-plate, fill one half of the pancake with the cooked liver mixture, then turn over the flap to make a half-moon of it, and serve hot. With a good surround of cooked vegetables, the filled pancake makes a substantial meal.

MIXED VEGETABLE DISHES

MIXED VEGETABLE CURRY

1 dessertspoon curry powder.
2 oz. dripping or cooking fat.
½ lb. home-grown tomatoes, or beetroot.
A bunch of spring onions (or 2-3 medium onions, if available).

1 lb. potatoes, sliced.
A few sprigs of raw cauliflower (or a whole small cauliflower divided into sprigs).
Fresh shelled peas or broad beans in season, or a few small sprouts.

Melt the fat in the frying pan and stir in the curry powder, and fry a short while to draw the flavour. Next add the sliced tomatoes and potatoes and the remaining vegetables, stirring to absorb the fat and draw the juices. Add a pinch of salt.

Cover down and cook gently, with an occasional stir,

until the vegetables are tender. There should be no need
to add liquid with a fair proportion of watery vegetables,
or root vegetables, in the varieties chosen.

Drain the vegetables and arrange on a hot dish, reduce
the liquor and, if liked, season with sweet pickle or home-
made chutney, as well as a good shaking of pepper. (Serve
with a surround of well-cooked and drained rice or creamy
mashed potato.)

SUMMER SUPPER DISH

1 cup of cooked green peas.	½ pint white sauce.
½ cup flaked cooked fish.	Seasoning.

Wheatmeal toast

Combine the flaked fish and green peas, with seasoning, and mix with ¼ pint of white sauce.

Make the white sauce with ½ pint of milk—diluted with
water or vegetable stock—1 tablespoon of flour and a
small piece of cooking fat or margarine. (See p. 115).

Heat the fish and green-pea mixture in the sauce, then
turn out for serving on hot slices of wheatmeal toast. Top
with a little finely chopped parsley.

DUTCH CASSEROLE

½ lb. cooked beetroot.	chopped spring onion, fried.
½ lb. cooked carrot.	½ tea cup cooked pearl barley.
A few dried plums, if available.	½ lb. cooked potato.
1 small minced onion, or	2 good-sized sour apples.

Layer the diced root vegetables in the casserole with
seasoning and raw apple, previously cut into small pieces,
and the minced onion.

Add the chopped fruit, and the barley. Sprinkle with
a few browned breadcrumbs, dot with a few pieces of
dripping or cooking fat in fine shavings, and place in a
hot oven to heat through for 15 minutes. In this time
the apple should be softened and the flavours well blended,
but a little stock can be run in to start the dish if liked.

Other vegetables can be used in season—replacing the
beetroot with green peas or brussel sprouts, but retaining
potato as the basis of the dish.

When it can be spared, a small grating of cheese, in
with the breadcrumbs, adds to the flavour.

BAKED VEGETABLE PLATTER

1 lb. potatoes.	2-3 lb. spinach.
1 lb. carrots.	Dripping.
1 lb. parsnips.	Salt, pepper.

Scrub all the root vegetables very thoroughly. Cut the

potatoes into slices about 1¼ inch thick and the carrots and parsnips in quarters. Dry them and sprinkle with salt.

Melt a piece of dripping about the size of an egg in a baking tin and place the vegetables into it, basting them well. Bake until tender and nicely browned—using a little more fat, if necessary, to keep them free.

Meanwhile prepare and cook the spinach so that it will be ready with the other vegetables. Drain thoroughly, season, and pour in a little of the fat from the root vegetables.

Serve on a hot shallow dish, piling the spinach in the centre, and alternate quarters of carrot and parsnip at each end, points towards the centre. Overlapping slices of potato at the sides.

If possible, sprinkle a suspicion of grated cheese on the spinach. Serve with brown gravy or a piquant sauce. (See p. 116.)

AUTUMN VEGETABLE PLATTER (Hot)

Choose a good selection of vegetables—such as :—

Broad beans, carrots, small potatoes, a small cauliflower, a few sprigs of watercress. | Mustard sauce or grated cheese (if you have it.)

Scrub the potatoes and carrots. Prepare and cook the broad beans, cauliflower sprigs, and potatoes, so that all are ready for dishing at the same time.

Meanwhile, grate the cleaned carrots, and wash and trim the cress. When the vegetables are nearly ready make ¾ pint of white sauce, using 3 dessertspoons of flour, a walnut of fat, and ¾ pint of milk or vegetable boilings. Flavour with mustard creamed with a little vinegar, or with grated cheese (about 2 dessertspoons or what can be spared).

Have ready a hot shallow dish in which the vegetables can be served in sections, and arrange the potatoes at each end, with the beans at the sides, dividing the two with lines of grated carrot. Pile the cauliflower sprigs in a circular heap to the centre, and decorate with chopped parsley. Arrange a few tufts of watercress for decoration.

NEST OF VEGETABLES IN POTATO RING

2-3 cups of mixed cooked root vegetables—carrot, celery, parsnip, swede, etc.
1 dessertspoon of minced onion.
1 oz dripping.

1 tablespoon flour.
½ pint vegetable boilings or household stock.
½ teaspoon vegetable extract.
Mashed potatoes.

1 teaspoon browned crumbs.

Melt the fat in a small saucepan. Add the onion and brown well. Stir in the flour and cook by heating moderately and allowing the mixture to bubble and spread.

Dissolve the vegetable extract in the vegetable stock, then add it to the pan, stirring until the sauce thickens. Season and mix in the vegetables previously diced or cut into neat sections.

Arrange hot mashed potatoes in a ring on a fireproof plate, pile the vegetable mixture in the centre, sprinkle with a few browned crumbs, and put into a fairly hot oven for a few minutes to reheat and crisp the potato ring to an appetising colour.

A few cooked peas or beans added to the vegetable mixture, when in season, convert the dish into a substantial meal.

VEGETABLE BON BORUE

1 breakfast cup each, curried vegetables and boiled rice mixed together.	1 thickish slice of wheatmeal bread, soaked in milk.
1 large egg.	½ pint milk.
	Salt, pepper.

Chop the curried vegetables and mix them with the rice. Soak the bread in a little milk, then beat up lightly with a fork. Mix into the curry and turn into a greased fireproof dish.

Beat up the egg, pour on the milk, season well with salt and pepper, and pour on to the curry mixture. Bake in a gentle oven for twenty-five to thirty minutes till nicely set and firm to the touch.

VEGETABLE FLAN

For the pastry.	*For the filling.*
4 oz. flour.	6 oz. cooked chopped spinach,
2 oz. cooked sieved potato.	or cabbage or carrot, or a
½ teaspoon baking powder.	good mixture of vegetables.
½ teaspoon salt.	½ oz. margarine.
1 oz. margarine.	½ oz. flour.
Cold water to mix.	½ pint milk.
Or, line the tin with stiff, well-mashed potato, bound with a very little beaten egg and milk.	2 teaspoons chopped parsley.

Line a flan tin with the pastry or stiff mashed potato. Prick it well over with a fork, and bake in a fairly hot oven from 20 to 30 minutes.

Melt the margarine, stir in the flour, and allow the

two to blend together for a minute or two. Add the milk gradually and allow to come to the boil, stirring smoothly. Season, and add the chopped parsley.

Stir in the vegetables, and when the pastry is cooked turn in the mixture, and garnish with the peas or grated carrot. Return to the oven for five to ten minutes, and serve very hot.

SUMMER VEGETABLE HOT-POT

1 lb. fresh peas.	Salt, pepper.
1½ lb. new potatoes.	¼ lb. runner beans.
Good bunch of spring onions.	½ lb. young turnips.
Small bunch fresh herbs.	Odd trimmings of bacon.
½ lb. young carrots.	2 tablespoons fine oatmeal.

Prepare the vegetables and, where suitable, cut them into slices, about ¼ inch in thickness. Place all the vegetables, except the peas, in a casserole or saucepan with sufficient stock or water to come half-way up the sides of the vegetables. Add salt, and a shake of pepper if liked. Place the bunch of herbs and the bacon trimmings on top, then cover closely and simmer for one hour.

Add the peas and the oatmeal, mixed to a smooth paste with a little water, stir well, and cook for another 20 minutes. Taste and add more salt and pepper if wished. Serve hot, with a sprinkling of chopped parsley.

ENGLISH GARDEN PIE

2 good-sized potatoes.	1 oz. dripping.
2 carrots.	A little grated nutmeg.
1 parsnip.	Salt and pepper.
3 tablespoons chopped spring onions.	A little thyme.
	A small bay leaf.
1 good teaspoon chopped parsley.	2 bacon rinds.
	½ pint vegetable stock.

Potato pastry.[1]

Scrub the vegetables, trim them and cut into neat slices. Chop the spring onions including the green.

Put the dripping in a frying pan with the bacon rinds to give additional flavour. The rinds should be chopped into small pieces.

When the fat and bacon rinds are heated through, put in the spring onions. When the onion starts to colour, add the carrots and fry quickly, then put in the parsnip and lastly the potato, frying and shaking the pan briskly over the heat for a few minutes.

[1] For recipe see page 59, POTATOES.

Season well with salt, pepper, a little grated nutmeg and a good teaspoon of chopped parsley.

Put the vegetable mixture into a pie-dish. When you have put half into the dish, add a little thyme and a small bay leaf.

Put in the rest of the vegetables and add a breakfastcup of cold vegetable boilings or water. Cover with potato pastry crust—using 3 oz. flour, 3 oz. mashed potato and 2½ oz. fat.

The above recipe may be varied according to the season and to the commodities available. A little minced liver or steak, a stick of celery, a flavouring of yeast extract in the gravy are some suggestions.

If you like plenty of gravy, make it separately and serve it in a sauceboat.

Enough for two people.

LORD WOOLTON PIE

The ingredients of this pie can be varied according to the vegetables in season.

Potato, swede, cauliflower and carrot make a good mixture.

Take 1 lb. of them, diced, 3 or 4 spring onions, if possible, 1 teaspoonful vegetable extract and 1 tablespoonful of oatmeal.

Cook altogether for 10 minutes with just enough water to cover. Stir occasionally to prevent the mixture from sticking.

Allow to cool, put into a pie-dish, sprinkle with chopped parsley and cover with a crust of potato or wheatmeal pastry.

Bake in a moderate oven until the pastry is nicely browned and serve hot with a brown gravy. Enough for 4 or 5.

If you are short of fat, use this pie-crust which is made without fat :

Mix together 8 ozs. wheatmeal flour,
1 level teaspoonful baking powder,
a pinch of salt,
a pinch of powdered sage if liked.

Stir in nearly ¼ pint of cold milk, or milk and water.

Roll out the mixture and use it as you would an ordinary crust, but serve the pie *hot*.

POTATOES

SOMEBODY ought to write a song in praise of the potato. It is cheap. It is nourishing. It is an Energy Food and a Protective Food. It can be cooked in an endless variety of interesting ways.

The potato does an all-round war-time job. It contains the valuable Vitamin C, the vitamin that we miss when fruit is scarce.

It can save us flour and fat when we use it in making cakes, scones, puddings and pastries. And medical advice encourages us each to eat 1 lb. of potatoes every day.

We should remember to cook them in their skins. Peeling is wasteful. It is easy to scrub them, steam them and remove the skins afterwards while they are hot. This brings out their flavour. Baked potatoes should be eaten in their jackets; the flavour of the jacket is very good.

The water in which potatoes have been boiled makes a useful foundation for soup. Left-over mashed potato can be used for thickening stews. Well-seasoned mashed potato, mixed with a little vegetable extract, finely chopped spring onions, chopped parsley, or meat makes an excellent sandwich filling.

EVERYDAY WAYS OF COOKING POTATOES

Before cooking, scrub the potatoes with a small brush under the running cold tap.

TO STEAM

Place the potatoes in a steamer. If you have not got one, use a colander over a pan of boiling water. Sprinkle them with salt, and steam for about 40 minutes to one hour, according to their size. Dry them directly over heat for a few minutes, then serve at once.

TO BOIL

Choose even-sized potatoes if possible, so that they will all be finished at the same time. Scrub them and place in boiling salted water. Bring the water back to the boil, then turn the heat low to cook them gently for 10 to 15 minutes. Drain off the water, place a folded cloth over the potatoes to cover them completely, put on the pan lid again, and let them cook in their own steam at the side of the hotplate for another 20 minutes.

TO MASH

After steaming into the folded cloth, the potatoes become floury, and the skins are easily removed. When completely dried, mash them thoroughly with a fork until free from lumps. Add a little hot milk, a little margarine if you can spare it, salt and pepper. Whip with the fork until very light, then pile into a heated dish.

TO ROAST

Choose medium-sized potatoes, scrub them well and cook them in boiling salted water for 10 minutes. Take them out, drain them, remove their skins, and place them in the baking tin beneath the meat for $\frac{3}{4}$ hour before the joint is to be ready. If you are not cooking a joint, place the potatoes in a baking tin in which you have melted a little dripping. Turn and baste the potatoes once or twice during cooking. When tender drain them on crumpled paper and sprinkle with salt before piling them in the hot vegetable dish.

TO BAKE IN THEIR JACKETS

Choose medium to large-sized potatoes for this, scrub and wash them thoroughly, then pat dry in a cloth. Place them in a baking tin, or on the oven shelf, in a well-heated oven, cooking them till tender—$\frac{3}{4}$ to one hour.

When soft, hold the potato in both hands with a cloth, squeeze it gently until it bursts, then return to the bottom of the oven for a minute or two. This lets the steam escape and makes it floury. Season with a very little pepper and salt.

TO FRY POTATOES (IF YOU MUST)

In war-time, to take up less fat, fry potatoes after cooking rather than when they are raw. Cut the cold potato into neat slices and fry in smoking hot dripping or cooking fat, turning until evenly crisped and brown. Sprinkle with salt and a little chopped parsley.

PARSLEY POTATO CAKES (for Breakfast)

1 lb. potatoes.	Browned breadcrumbs.
Tablespoon chopped parsley.	Frying fats (optional).

Save 1 lb. of cooked potatoes when you are cooking, the day before you want to make the cakes. Mash these while hot, with a little hot milk, and seasoning of salt and pepper to taste.

Next day add a tablespoon of chopped parsley and shape the mixture into little cakes. Cover these with browned breadcrumbs, and pan-fry in a little hot fat, or bake in the oven. The mixture should be firm and dry.

POTATO FLODDIES (Pancakes)

2 good-sized potatoes.　　　　Seasoning.
Flour to form a batter.　　　　Frying fat.

Scrub the potatoes and grate them into a bowl. Then add sufficient flour to form a batter. There is no need to add any liquid. Season with salt and pepper.

Melt a little dripping or frying fat, and make it very hot in a frying pan. Drop the mixture into it, and when brown on one side, turn and brown on the other.

Add a pinch of mixed herbs and a dash of cayenne pepper to the recipe if you want it more savoury. Serve it plain with jam if you want it as a sweet dish.

POTATO OVEN SCONES

4 oz. mashed potato.　　　　4-5 tablespoons milk.
6 oz. plain flour.　　　　$\frac{1}{2}$ teaspoon salt.
2 level teaspoons baking powder.　　　1 oz. fat.

Sift the flour, salt, and baking powder into a basin. Mix thoroughly with the potato. Rub in the fat with the tips of the fingers, and blend into a soft dough with the milk. Roll out to $\frac{1}{2}$ inch thickness, cut into small rounds and glaze the tops with milk. Bake on greased baking sheets in a hot oven for 15 minutes.

Variations

For a sweet scone—add 1 oz. sugar.

Coffee scones—add 1 oz. sugar and 1 teaspoon of coffee essence blended with slightly less milk.

Fillings

DEVONSHIRE SPLIT (sweet or coffee)

(1) Jam and whisked substitute cream.
(2) Add cocoa or chocolate powder and a little milk to creamed margarine.

SAVOURY SPLIT (plain)

(1) Equal parts of grated raw carrot and grated raw cabbage bound with chutney.
(2) Cooked beetroot grated into sharp sauce (white sauce vinegar or chopped pickle).
(3) Celery mayonnaise.
(4) Watercress " butter " (chopped watercress and creamed margarine).

POTATO TOPPINGS FOR TOAST

Cover slices of wheatmeal toast with one of the following mixtures, and crisp them under the grill.

(1) Freshly cooked mashed potato, blended with a little milk and meat or vegetable extract to taste. Season, dot with tiny pieces of margarine or dripping and brown under the grill.

(2) Arrange alternately some thin slices of cooked potato and raw tomato when in season. Dot with dripping or margarine, season well, and replace under the grill until the potatoes are brown and the tomatoes cooked. Sprinkle with finely chopped parsley.

(3) Mix some puree potato with half the quantity of flaked fish. Season well, add some chopped parsley, or a dash of anchovy essence or ketchup. Spread the mixture evenly on the slices of toast, dot with fat, and brown under the grill.

IRISH POTATO CAKES

½ lb. mashed potatoes.	I teaspoon salt.
I small teacupful milk.	I oz. margarine.
½ lb. flour.	I½ teaspoons baking powder.

Sift flour, baking powder, and salt into a basin. Rub in the margarine, then mix in the mashed potatoes and milk by degrees. Stir until smooth, and turn on to a lightly floured board. Roll out to ¼ inch thickness, and cut into rounds.

Fry in a little smoking fat until brown on both sides, or cook on a solid metal hotplate or hot girdle.

FADGE (Irish Potato Bread)

Scrub and boil 2 lbs. of potatoes. Drain and dry over a low heat. Mash with a fork while still hot. Allow to cool until the little finger can bear the heat of the potato. Add salt and work in enough flour to make a pliable dough. Knead well for about 5 minutes on a heavily floured board. Roll out about ¼ inch thick. Cut into wedge-shaped pieces. Cook on a hotplate or hot girdle or in the oven until brown. Turn and brown the other side.

POTATO AND FISH CAKES

8 oz. hot mashed potatoes.	1 teaspoon chopped parsley.
4 oz. flaked cooked fish.	1 small teacup milk and
A little frying fat.	water.
Baked breadcrumbs.	1 tablespoon flour.
Salt and pepper.	1 oz. cooking fat or dripping.

Melt 1 oz. fat in a pan, mix in the flour smoothly, cook for a minute or two and then add the milk and water gradually, stirring well. Boil for 10 minutes.

Flake the fish free from bone with a fork into a basin. Add the potatoes, sauce, parsley and salt and pepper to taste. Form into a square and set aside to cool. Shape into 6 or 8 round cakes, sprinkle with the breadcrumbs, patting them in well. Fry in a little smoking hot fat on both sides until golden brown. Serve on a hot dish garnished with parsley. (See also FISH CAKES, p. 75.)

POTATO AND VEGETABLE PIE

1 lb. raw potatoes	1 tablespoon finely chopped
1 lb. mixed vegetables.	spring onion.
Salt and Pepper.	1 oz. dripping, stock or gravy.

Combinations of any of the following vegetables may be used :—carrots, peas, turnips, swedes, parsnips, tomatoes, according to season. Dried vegetables like haricot or butter beans should be previously soaked and cooked.

Chop the onion finely, dice the root vegetables with the exception of the potatoes, which should be cut into slices. Combine all the other vegetables, season well, and place in a pie-dish. Half fill with stock or vegetable water.

Cover the pie with overlapping slices of raw potato, dot with dripping and cover with a margarine wrapper. Bake for 1¼ hours in a moderate oven, removing the paper for the last quarter of an hour for the potato circles to crisp and brown.

SUPPER CASSEROLE

1 lb. potatoes. 1 oz. fat.	*Dumpling mixture :*
½ lb. carrots.	2 oz. fine oatmeal, 2 oz. plain
1 quart of stock or water.	flour, 1½ oz. dripping or
A little chopped spring onion.	chopped suet, level tea-
1 level teaspoon mixed herbs.	spoon finely chopped par-
1 level teaspoon chopped par-	sley, pinch baking powder,
sley.	pinch of mixed herbs, cold
Salt and pepper.	water to mix.

Scrub and grate the potatoes and carrots (do not scrape them), finely chop the onion. Heat the fat in a saucepan, add the vegetables and stir them over a low flame for a few minutes. Add the water or stock, herbs and chopped parsley. Season with salt and pepper, and simmer gently for 15-20 minutes, stirring frequently.

To make a supper meal—make a few savoury dumplings to cook in the stew. Sift the flour and baking powder with a small pinch of salt and rub in the soft fat, if it is to be used. Then add the oatmeal, seasonings, herbs, etc., and if chopped suet is used in place of dripping, it should be added now.

Mix to a firm dough with cold water, divide into eight pieces and, with floured fingers, form it into balls. Add these to the casserole about half an hour before it is to be served, cooking with the lid in position throughout.

POTATO PIGLETS

6 medium well-crubbed pota- Cooked cabbage—lightly
   toes.   chopped.
6 skinned sausages.

Make a hole lengthwise through the centre of each potato, using an apple corer, and stuff the cavity with sausage meat. Bake in the usual way and arrange the piglets on a bed of cooked cabbage. (The potato removed from the centres is useful for soup.)

JACK-IN-THE-BOX

Substitute sprats, when in season, for sausage meat—in the foregoing recipe—allowing 2 sprats for each potato. Make one head emerge from one side and the tail of the second fish appear from the other end of the tunnel. Bake as before and serve on a bed of cabbage dressed with a little vinegar, a grating of nutmeg and a good shake of pepper.

POTATO BASKET

1 lb. potatoes.	$\frac{1}{2}$ pint stock or milk.
1 lb. carrots.	1 egg.
1 oz. oatmeal.	Salt, pepper.
1 oz. dripping.	Browned crumbs.

Scrub the potatoes and boil them gently in a very little water. When they are nearly cooked, drain off the liquid, reserving it for stock. Let them finish cooking in their own steam, covering closely with a folded cloth under the lid and standing at the side of the stove until floury.

Remove the skins and mash well. Add the beaten egg and mash again, adding salt and pepper.

Grease a cake tin and coat it with browned bread-crumbs. Press in the mashed potatoes to form a thick lining to the tin. Bake in a hot oven for 15-20 minutes.

Meanwhile dice the carrots, cook them for 15 minutes, and mix them with a sauce made from the fat, oatmeal, and liquid, adding pepper and salt to taste.

When the potato basket is cooked, turn it out and fill it with the carrot mixture. Place it in the oven for a few minutes and serve piping hot, with a sprinkling of finely chopped parsley.

SCOTS POTATO PIES

Large, well-scrubbed potatoes.	Stock or milk.
Scraps of cooked meat.	Ketchup or piquant sauce.
Chopped parsley, mixed herbs.	Salt and pepper.

Scrub the potatoes, then cut off a slice lengthwise, and hollow out the centre of the potatoes with a teaspoon, leaving at least $\frac{1}{2}$ inch all over. Mince the meats, or chop them finely, and mix with the potato, which has been scooped away and finely chopped, the parsley and herbs. Season well, add a dash of ketchup and moisten with stock. A little minced onion or chopped spring onion can be added for flavour.

Stuff the " pies " with this mixture, replace the tops, and bake in a moderate oven until the potatoes are cooked and the " walls " softened. Serve with a good brown gravy.

BAKED POTATOES (Stuffed)

Large baked potatoes can be stuffed in a great variety of ways. Here are a few suggestions :—

(1) Cut the potato in half lengthwise, scoop out most of the inside and mix in a basin with about 4 ozs. of cooked meat or fish, finely chopped and loosened with a little sauce or gravy. Season with salt and pepper, pile into the potato cases, sprinkle with chopped parsley and reheat in the oven.

(2) Mix the scooped-out potato with pepper and salt and a little cheese to taste. Pile into the potato cases, sprinkle the tops with a little more grated cheese, and return to the oven to brown.

(3) Mix the potato with any finely cut left-over cooked vegetables, and proceed as before.

(4) Whip the pureed potato with sufficient vegetable

extract to flavour, and return to the cases, for quick heating through.

(5) Make a lengthwise slit in a baked potato. Place a par-boiled sausage in the opening and return the potato to the oven until the sausage is cooked.

PICCANINNIES

Scrub a large potato well and bake in its jacket till soft. Cut in half lengthwise, scoop out the centre and mix with any of the following fillings. Pile up in one half of the potato jacket, put the other half on top and tilt to show the filling. Replace in the oven to heat through.

Fillings—

(1) Equal quantities of cooked shredded cabbage, diced carrot and turnip, bound with white sauce and flavoured with a dash of piquant sauce.

(2) Roughly chopped dry fried sprats, bound with mustard sauce.

(3) Shredded raw cabbage and chopped parsley, bound with mayonnaise.

POTATO AND SPINACH CROQUETTES

1 lb. freshly mashed potato.	Thick sauce — 1 tablespoon
½ cup finely chopped cooked spinach.	flour, 1 oz. dripping, 1 gill milk (see p. 115).
Salt and pepper.	Browned crumbs.
Grate of nutmeg.	

Make the sauce, add potatoes and spinach and season well. Spread on a wet plate and set aside to cool. When cold, divide into six or eight equal-sized portions.

Roll in browned crumbs, and bake in a hot oven for 15 minutes.

MIDDLETON MEDLEY

Beat some mashed potato with a little milk, including a little egg if possible. Pipe with forcing bag, or mould with a fork into little nest shapes. Bake these in a hot oven for 15 minutes until lightly browned. Fill with one of the following fillings :—

(1) Diced cooked carrots and turnips, with a sprinkling of finely chopped parsley.

(2) Small cooked sprouts sprinkled with finely grated cheese or ground mixed nuts. Substitute spinach when in season.

CHAMP

Potatoes.
Margarine or dripping.
A little milk.
Either cabbage, carrots or other root vegetables, peas, beans,
chives or spring onion, parsley or nettles, according to season. Or a mixture of two or three.

Cook a large pan of potatoes, allowing them to steam off and dry in the usual way. Cook the selected vegetable in very little water (with the lid on).

Peel and mash the potatoes, beating well, then pour in a little milk, add seasoning of pepper and salt, then the cooked vegetable. Serve piping hot on hot plates, with a small pat of margarine or dripping on each portion.

SCALLOPED POTATOES

1 lb. potatoes.
1 tablespoon flour.
½ pint milk, or half milk half vegetable stock.
A few breadcrumbs.
Chopped parsley, sliced spring onion, or chopped celery, to taste.
Salt and pepper to taste.

Scrub and scrape the potatoes, then cut them into fairly thin slices. Arrange the layers in a pie dish or casserole, sprinkling each layer with seasoned flour. Layer with a little chopped parsley and the minced celery or onion. Pour in the milk, sprinkle the top with breadcrumbs or raspings. Bake in a moderate oven for about one hour, or cook in a frying pan covered with a plate for ½ to ¾ hour over low heat.

SAVOURY SURPRISES

8 oz. plain flour.
2 oz. fat.
4 oz. cooked potato.
½ teaspoon salt.

Sieve the flour and salt into a basin. Rub in the fat, add the potato and bind together with a little cold water to a dry dough. Roll out about ¼ inch thick and cut into rounds with a saucer. Pile any of the suggested fillings (see below) into the centre of the pastry rounds, brush the edges with water and mould into dumplings. Bake in a hot oven 15 minutes.

Fillings—
(1) Canned salmon mixed with parsley, seasoned with salt and pepper and bound with a little sauce.
(2) Oatmeal sauce, made with ½ oz. dripping, ½ oz. fine oatmeal, ¼ pt. stock, flavoured with 1 teaspoon of

vegetable extract and a variety of diced cooked vegetables (carrots, turnips, sprouts, celery, etc.).

PINK AND GREEN PUREE

I lb. freshly cooked potatoes. | Salt and pepper.
I large carrot. | Milk.
I small bunch watercress. | A small piece of fat.

Mash the potato while it is hot, add a little milk and a small piece of margarine or dripping if it can be spared. Whip to a puree with a fork. Scrub and grate the carrot. Wash and chop the watercress. Add both to the puree potato, season well, reheat for a few minutes and pile pyramid fashion in a vegetable dish.

POTATO BISCUITS

2 oz. dry mashed potato. | 4 oz. flour.
I oz. margarine or cooking fat. | Pinch salt.
I oz. sugar. | $\frac{1}{4}$ teaspoon baking powder.
Beaten egg, or milk, for mixing.

Sieve flour, baking powder and salt. Rub in the fat evenly, then the potato. Add the sugar and mix all to a stiff dough with the egg and milk.

Roll out to $\frac{1}{8}$ inch thickness and cut into an even number of rounds. Remove the centres from half the number of biscuits with a small cutter. Bake the biscuits in a moderate oven, till crisp and light coloured, allow to cool, then spread the whole ones with jam. Place the biscuit rings on top to show the jam in the centre.

POTATO SALADS

(*See page* 60, SALADS.)

For use in salads, either new potatoes or the waxy varieties are most suitable. The golden rule is, " Mix warm and eat cold."

Steam the potatoes in their skins, then peel and cut them into dice for the dressing. If you have a little mashed potato left from the previous day, try whipping it to a thick creamy consistency with a little mayonnaise dressing, and arranging it in the centre of a green salad. It makes the dressing go further.

POTATO SALAD

Steam 1 lb. potatoes in their skins, peel and cut them into small dice. Add a finely chopped pickled onion and salad dressing, whatever kind you like best. Mix these together well with a wooden spoon. When the salad is cold add a good sprinkling of chopped parsley.

To make a more substantial serving—add neatly cut rings of cooked sausage—one sausage for each person.

HOT POTATO SALAD

Cook potatoes in their jackets. When ready, peel them and cut into neat slices. Have ready a dressing of pepper, salt, a little sugar, mustard, oil if possible, hot milk and lastly a little vinegar.

Mix the potatoes thoroughly with the dressing, and add some chopped parsley, or, if you have any, a little chopped onion. Serve hot, in a hot dish.

SUNSET SALAD

Save your orange peel for this, and when you have some hot mashed potato mix into it a little grated orange rind. Quickly beat it in until thoroughly blended, when the mixture takes on a pretty pinky-orange colour.

Whip creamy with a little vinaigrette or mock-mayonnaise and include a little grated or finely chopped celery, or spring onion. Pile on to a bed of grated cabbage or broken lettuce, and decorate with a few sprigs of heart celery or centre green tufts. A few sprigs of watercress make an attractive contrast of colour.

CARROT-CAP SALAD

Cook two to three good-sized potatoes in their skins. When tender, strain without drying off, to avoid making them floury. Slice and dice them neatly ; then dress in vinaigrette dressing (two parts salad oil to one of vinegar, pepper and salt to taste) while they are still hot.

Pile in a salad bowl lined with a few shredded lettuce leaves or watercress. Sprinkle with a little chopped chive or rings of spring onion, and pile high with grated carrot.

To make a more substantial dish, add one or two boned sardines or fillets of smoked herring.

RADISH AND POTATO SALAD

Cold cooked potatoes.	Lettuce.
A few full-colour red radishes.	Cooked green peas.

Mayonnaise or French dressing.

Carefully dice the potatoes, choosing waxy or new ones if possible. Wash and prepare the radishes and cut them into slices. Mix the potatoes and radishes lightly with mayonnaise or dressing and pile on crisp lettuce leaves. Arrange an outer border of cooked peas, and sprinkle the centre with a little chopped parsley.

POTATO SOUP

I lb. potatoes.	1½ pints water or vegetable boilings.
½ pint milk.	
I oz. margarine or dripping.	I onion or leek or stick of celery.
I tablespoon of flour.	
Salt and pepper.	Chopped parsley.

Melt the fat in the saucepan, peel and slice the potatoes and onion, and cook gently in the fat for 10 minutes. Cover the saucepan and shake the contents from time to time.

Add the stock or water and cook until the vegetables are tender, then rub them through a sieve, or break up with a spoon.

Blend the flour with a little milk, add some of the soup, and return all to the pan, stirring until the mixture boils. Add the rest of the milk, season to taste, heat through, and serve with a sprinkling of finely chopped parsley.

POTATO AND WATERCRESS SOUP

Scrub a pound of potatoes and cut them into quarters. Boil these in 1½ pints of water until soft. Then pass them through a sieve, return to the pan, add one bunch of watercress (washed and shredded) and pepper and salt to taste. Simmer very gently for 5 minutes, adding a little milk if too thick. (Enough for three or four).

POTATO AND LEEK SOUP

6 small scrubbed potatoes.	I gill milk and water.
3 leeks.	Salt, pepper.
1½-2 pints vegetable boilings.	Very small pinch of mace, or grated nutmeg.
I oz. fat.	
I oz. flour.	A little fat for frying.

Slice the leeks very thinly and fry them in a very little fat until lightly browned. Add the finely chopped potatoes, then cook for a few minutes without colouring, adding salt.

Pour on the stock and allow to simmer gently, with the pan covered, for about one hour. Make up a thick panada sauce with 1 oz. each of fat and flour, and a gill of milk and water, then pour on some of the hot soup to slacken to pouring consistency. Return all to the saucepan, stirring as it comes to the boil. Season well with pepper and salt, and serve piping hot.

POTATO AND MIXED VEGETABLE SOUP

3 medium-sized potatoes.
I oz. flour.
I breakfastcup of cooked vege-
    tables.
Carrots, turnips, peas, or spin-
    ach, etc.

I oz. fat.
I tablespoon minced onion, or
    chopped spring onion.
¾ pint potato stock.
½ pint household stock.
¾ pint of milk and water.

Boil the potatoes in the usual way, then drain and reserve the liquid for stock. Sieve the potatoes and add them to the pan, together with the onion and other cooked vegetable and measured stock.

Simmer slowly in a covered pan for 20 minutes to ½ hour. Make a binding sauce with the fat and flour, adding the measured milk slowly till the mixture thickens. Combine this sauce with the hot soup, season and serve.

For this soup any sieved cooked vegetable may be used, or a combination of vegetables in season.

SURPRISE POTATO BALLS

I lb. cooked potato.
I large carrot, grated.
I teaspoon chopped parsley.
A little sweet pickle.

Salt and pepper.
A few teaspoons of milk, if
    necessary.
Browned breadcrumbs.

Cook the potatoes and beat them well with a fork. Add the grated carrot, parsley, salt and pepper. Use a little milk, if necessary, to bind the mixture, but do not make it wet. Form into balls. Make a hole in each, drop in a small spoonful of pickle and close the hole.

Roll in the breadcrumbs, place on a greased baking sheet, and cover with a margarine paper. Bake in a really hot oven for 15-20 minutes. Serve piping hot with good gravy.

POTATO WAFFLES

2 oz. mashed potato.
4 oz. plain flour.
½ egg or egg substitute.
I small teaspoon cream of tartar.

I level teaspoon bicarbonate of
    soda.
¼ teaspoon salt.
I gill milk.

Sieve the flour and salt and rub in the mashed potato. Make into a stiff batter with the egg, or egg substitute, and milk. Allow to stand for a time. Just before cooking sift in the cream of tartar and bicarbonate of soda. Cook on a waffle iron, or in spoonfuls on a hot, lightly greased girdle or frying pan, turning to cook both sides evenly.

Serve with—

(1) Flaked fish creamed with a little caper sauce (see p. 115).

(2) Diced carrot cooked in curry sauce.

Waffles, served with suitable toppings of chopped fresh fruits, or diced apple with honey, etc., can make a good sweet.

DEVILLED POTATOES

1 lb. cold cooked potatoes.	1 saltspoon dry mustard.
1 level dessertspoon curry powder.	A shake of cayenne pepper.
	Salt.
1 level dessertspoon flour.	A little fat for frying.

Cut the potatoes in slices about $\frac{1}{4}$ inch thick. Put the curry powder in a frying pan and shake it over low heat for a few minutes to bring out the flavour. Turn on to a plate, add the flour, mustard, cayenne and a little salt and blend thoroughly. Dip the slices of potato in this mixture and fry in a little hot fat on both sides. Sprinkle with vinegar and serve at once.

SWEET POTATO PUDDING

Rind of $\frac{1}{2}$ orange and two sticks diced rhubarb, or a few first gooseberries from the garden.	8 oz. sieved cooked potatoes.
	Level teaspoon salt.
	2 oz. cooking fat.
	1 egg.
2 dessertspoons honey.	

Mix all the ingredients together and beat well, turning in the diced fruit last of all. Place in a fireproof dish, and bake in a moderate oven for about $\frac{3}{4}$ hour.

POTATO STUFFING

1 lb. hot mashed potato.	Salt and pepper to taste.
1 oz. dripping.	A little chopped spring onion.
1 tablespoon parsley.	$\frac{1}{2}$ teaspoon mixed herbs.
A little milk.	

Put the hot potato and dripping into a basin and beat together until the dripping has melted. Add remaining ingredients and a little milk.

For a delicious roast use this recipe to stuff a boned breast of mutton or brisket of beef.

POTATO BREAD

1 lb. cooked sieved potato.	1 oz. cooking fat.
1 lb. plain flour.	$1\frac{1}{2}$ teaspoons salt.
$\frac{1}{4}$ oz. yeast.	$\frac{1}{4}$ teaspoon sugar.
$\frac{3}{4}$ pint warm water.	

Sift the flour and salt together and run in the cooking fat. Add the potato and break up finely with the flour.

Make a well in the centre of the flour mixture, and pour in the yeast creamed with the sugar and with ½ pint warm water. Sprinkle some of the flour mixture over the liquid and put the basin in a warm place until the yeast has sponged through. Add sufficient warm water to make a light dough. Knead well with floured hands, put into a warm place to rise to double the original size. Again knead well, turning the dough on to a pastry board as soon as it leaves the sides of the basin. Divide into two portions. Place into 1-lb. bread tins and allow to prove in a warm place for 30 minutes. Bake in a hot oven for about 1 to 1¼ hours.

POTATO PASTRY

8 oz. sieved cooked potatoes.	½ teaspoon salt.
4 oz. flour.	2 oz. cooking fat.

Sieve the flour with the salt. Rub the fat into the flour, using the tips of the fingers, until the whole has the appearance of fine breadcrumbs. Add the potato and rub lightly into the other ingredients. Mix to a very dry dough with a small quantity of cold water. Knead well with the fingers and roll out. This may be used for either sweet or savoury dishes.

POTATO SUET CRUST

8 oz. flour.	Salt.
2 oz. grated raw potato.	Water to mix.
2 oz. suet (finely chopped).	Level teaspoon baking powder.

Mix the ingredients and cook in the usual way. This recipe saves suet yet makes a light crust.

WAR AND PEACE CHRISTMAS PUDDING

This pudding was made in Canada during the last war. It makes a good war-time Christmas pudding.

Mix together 1 cupful of flour, 1 cupful of breadcrumbs, half a cupful of suet, half a cupful of mixed dried fruit, and, if you like, a teaspoonful of mixed sweet spice. Then add a cupful of grated raw potato, a cupful of grated raw carrot, and finally a level teaspoonful of bicarbonate of soda dissolved in two tablespoonfuls of hot water. Mix all together, turn into a well-greased pudding bowl. The bowl should not be more than two-thirds full. Boil or steam for at least 2 hours.

SALADS

SIMPLE SALAD

1 crisp lettuce.	Cupful of cooked diced potatoes.
1 carrot.	Vinaigrette.
1 apple.	Chopped mint.

A small chopped onion, if possible.

Wash and examine carefully a crisp lettuce, then drain and crisp between the folds of a clean towel. Place the leaves in a bowl and dress them in vinaigrette made from 2 tablespoons of salad oil, 1 tablespoon of vinegar, and salt and pepper seasoning.

Turn the leaves well in the dressing, then drain and line the bowl with them, reserving the heart for garnish. Pile in the centre the cooked diced potatoes (also dressed in vinaigrette if liked), surround with the chopped apple, and grate the carrot lightly over the potatoes in the centre. Decorate the apple with finely chopped mint, and sprinkle the carrot top with the minced onion.

CAULIFLOWER SALAD

Springs of cooked cauliflower.	Tomato slices, or rings of
Sliced cooked potato.	radish.

Chopped parsley. | Crisped lettuce. | Oil and vinegar.

Dress the sprigs of cauliflower in vinaigrette dressing, and drain. Dressed lettuce is then arranged on the dish with slices of cooked potato, fringing the edge. Tip with a touch of mayonnaise dressing on the circles of the potato, unless there is sufficient to dress them entirely. Decorate with rings of tomato or radish, and arrange the cauliflower in the centre, with a sprinkling of chopped parsley.

UNCOOKED CAULIFLOWER SALAD

1 cauliflower.	Chopped parsley.
Equal quantity of radish.	1 tablespoon of thick mayon-
Crisp lettuce leaves.	naise.

A few sprigs watercress

Grate the uncooked flower of a cauliflower and mix with an equal quantity of grated radish. Pile on a prepared bed of crisped broken lettuce, and smaller lettuce leaves, and sprinkle with chopped parsley. Edge with a few sprigs of watercress for contrast.

WINTER SALAD

1 teacup of chopped cooked meat, mixed with 4 cooked potatoes, sliced thinly.	Heart of a raw cabbage, sliced.
	Sprigs of watercress.
	Chopped celery and raw beet-
$\frac{1}{2}$ teacup of cooked diced carrots.	root ($\frac{1}{2}$ teacup each).

Mix the chopped meat with the thinly sliced cooked potatoes and the diced carrots. Line a salad bowl with the finely sliced heart of raw cabbage, and pile the meat and vegetable mixture in the centre.

Round this arrange neat heaps of chopped celery and beetroot, arranged alternately, previously dressed in oil and vinegar dressing. Fringe the edge of the dish with a little watercress, and sprinkle the top with finely chopped parsley.

BROAD BEAN SALAD

Either raw or cooked, broad beans are excellent in salad. Sprinkle raw young beans with a little salt and include them in a French salad of garden greens. Cold cooked broad beans are also good, and add to the food value. They should be skinned before they are added to the salad.

FRENCH BEAN SALAD

For a good salad with tomatoes, allow double the quantity of tomatoes to that of French beans. Have the beans cooked, and when they are quite cold, cut into short lengths or " straws " and dress with vinaigrette dressing, using double measure salad oil to vinegar.

Arrange peeled tomato in slices, with a sprinkling of minced onion, or diced spring onion, if liked. Heap the dressed beans in neat piling in the centre of the dish.

FRENCH BEAN AND FISH SALAD (Hot)

Herrings and all oily fish are good with beans. Sauté $\frac{1}{2}$ pint of cooked French beans in a little fat, frying them until beginning to brown. Pile in the centre of the heated dish and sprinkle with freshly chopped parsley.

Arrange soused herrings round the outer section of the dish, one for each person. Finally fringe the edge of the dish with hot potato salad. (See page 55, POTATO chapter.)

JUNE SALAD

Fresh crisp lettuce, with good heart.
A few leaves of spinach.
10 or 12 strawberries.
A little cooked rice blended in mayonnaise.
Mustard and cress.

Wash and drain the salad plants, crisping them between the folds of a clean towel, or on a sieve or colander lined with a cloth.

Arrange a bed of dressed lettuce in the salad bowl,

then open out the centre heart by loosening the leaves, and setting it on the dish. Arrange a ring of mayonnaise-blended rice to support the heart, and a small spoonful in the centre of the lettuce, then split the strawberries with a sharp fruit knife, pepper them slightly, and cup a few in the heart. Arrange the rest on the rice border.

Chop the cleaned spinach to give a dark contrast round the base of the rice and place the washed cress in bunches at the edge of the dish.

TURNIP SALAD (Cooked)

Cold boiled turnips are appetising if used this way. Slice or dice the vegetable, blend with a little salad dressing, and pile in a small salad dish. Edge with sliced beetroot, and top with a bunch of watercress.

TURNIP SALAD (Hot Snack)

Newly cooked turnips make an interesting dish this way. Prepare a round of wheatmeal toast, and spread while hot with anchovy paste, or fish-flavoured paste, blended with a very little fat.

Cut the turnips into blocks or slices, and blend in a little well-seasoned parsley sauce (plain white sauce to which finely chopped parsley is added just before serving).

Place on the toast, and serve very hot.

CELERY LEAF SALAD

Wash and dry young celery leaves, leaving them to crisp a little. Toss them lightly in vinaigrette dressing —two parts salad oil to one of vinegar, with seasoning— and serve with diced beetroot, or grated raw beetroot, according to taste.

This makes a good accompaniment to a cold potato salad dressed with mayonnaise.

CELERY RELISH

Mix together equal quantities of raw apple (preferably red skinned) and raw celery, both chopped and shredded.

Soak in a dressing made of : two parts oil, 1 part vinegar, salt, pepper, and enough dry mustard to impart a " hot " flavour.

Marinate long enough to absorb the dressing, and serve as accompaniment to less flavoured foods—sliced cold meats, etc.

DANDELION SALAD

1 pint dandelion leaves.	Diced cooked beetroot.

Vinaigrette dressing.

Wash and pick over the leaves thoroughly, then dry between the folds of a towel. Mix a vinaigrette dressing using two parts salad oil to one of vinegar, adding salt and pepper to taste. When crisped, dress the leaves with the vinaigrette and arrange in the salad bowl. Dice the cooked beetroot and pass through the dressing before arranging it in neat heaps at the edge of the bowl.

To vary the salad, take half a pint of young dandelion leaves, and the remaining measure in fresh lettuce.

CHICORY SALAD

It is not always appreciated that chicory makes a most attractive raw salad. Trim the vegetable, and leave it to crisp in cold water for about an hour. Then drain it well, and cut into thinnish strips.

Have a few pieces of diced spring onion placed in the bowl, then add the dressed chicory.

If preferred, the dressing can be poured over the chicory, and left to impregnate, with occasional stirring, for about 20 minutes before serving.

POTATO AND CELERIAC SALAD

To 1½ lb. potatoes allow 1 celeriac.	¾ gill of mayonnaise, or mock mayonnaise sauce.

Salt and pepper to taste.

Steam the potatoes in their jackets, then strip away the skins and cut into neat dice, dressing with vinaigrette dressing. Wash and peel the celeriac, trim into strips and dress in the mayonnaise, mixing part in with the potatoes. Arrange the remaining celeriac salad on top of the mounded salad in the dish, decorate with watercress sprigs or a little chopped parsley, and serve.

VEGETABLE BRAWN

2 pints of diced cooked vegetables (carrots, swedes, potatoes, beetroots, cauliflower).	1 hard-boiled egg (optional).
2 dessertspoons of chopped spring onions.	1 pint of liquid in which the vegetables have been cooked. (They can be diced and cooked all together, but put the cauliflower in about 5 minutes after the other vegetables.)
2 teaspoons vegetable extract.	
1 dessertspoon Worcester sauce or mushroom ketchup.	
Salt and pepper.	1 oz. gelatine.

Melt the gelatine and vegetable extract in a little of the hot vegetable liquid. Stir into the rest of the liquid with the seasoning and sauce.

If you can spare an egg, it will add to the food value and improve the appearance of the dish. Slice the egg and arrange it at the bottom of a wetted mould.

Now add your diced vegetables carefully to the liquid and stir gently in order not to break or mash them. Put them into the mould and leave in a cool place to set firmly.

Turn out and serve on a bed of salad. A garnishing of watercress is an improvement. The brawn makes a pleasant serving with wheatmeal bread and butter and a separate potato salad. As seasons change, use different vegetables. Add fresh peas, beans, diced cucumber or sliced tomato.

Vary the flavour sometimes. Finely chopped parsley may be added just before the vegetables are poured into the mould, or you may give the brawn quite a different flavour by adding mint or a dessertspoon of mint sauce.

Celery salt or a very small suspicion of pounded garlic are other suggestions for flavouring.

SALAD DRESSINGS

MAYONNAISE (Economical)

1 oz. flour.	1 oz. margarine or cooking fat.
1 teaspoon dry mustard.	½ pint milk.
2 tablespoons salad oil.	Vinegar to taste.

Make a coating sauce with the flour and mustard, fat and milk. Then allow to cool, with occasional stirring, before whisking in the salad oil. Season well and add sufficient vinegar to refresh and give a tartness.

EGGLESS MAYONNAISE

1 small teaspoon mustard.	1 small baked potato, or one
Salt.	steamed floury in its jacket.
A little vinegar.	Scant gill salad oil.

Peel and mash the potato, stir in mustard and salt, then add the vinegar gradually, beating well. Last of all beating in the salad oil slowly, mixing well.

WAR-TIME VINAIGRETTE

Mix together smoothly a pinch of dry mustard, a good shake of pepper and pinch of salt, with 2 dessertspoons of salad oil. Then add 4 dessertspoons of vinegar, gradually, dropping it from a teaspoon and stirring all the time.

HOME GROWN HERBS

A SMALL patch of garden or a window-box will provide enough space for all the herbs you need to grow. You will find them invaluable for flavouring war-time dishes. Remember to dry and store a supply for the winter.

PARSLEY

Raw parsley has real food value. It is very rich in Vitamins A and C, and contains iron.

Although it is an annual which you grow from seed, you can get an all-the-year-round crop by sowing some at the end of March and more again at the end of July.

Years ago country cottagers used to make parsley baskets and hang them in the doorway or porch. To do this, line a wire basket with moss and fill the centre with good soil. Insert the parsley roots through the crevices into the soil. When they are in full leaf, the hanging basket looks like a green feathery ball.

Add well-chopped parsley to every kind of dish from scrambled eggs and omelets to soups and stews. Use plenty of it in white sauces.

Baked potatoes with parsley sauce alone are delicious. Sprinkle chopped parsley on salads and on new potatoes.

Serve small parsley jellies with a fish salad, and use chopped parsley for flavouring fish cakes or rissoles.

When making a parsley sauce, remember to add the chopped parsley at the very last.

BAY LEAF

Bay leaves are excellent for flavouring white sauce, for the braising of celery, or as an added flavour to boiled carrots. Always use a leaf, or the part of one, when braising meat or vegetables, or when cooking oily fish such as mackerel or herring in vinegar. A small piece, used instead of the inevitable clove, improves bread sauce. Some people enjoy the flavour of bay leaf in custard or milk pudding.

When home-grown tomatoes are available, make a savoury dish with them lightly fried with a small piece of garlic and half a bay leaf blended with boiled rice.

THYME (Lemon flavoured and Black varieties)

This herb makes a great improvement in all stuffings for veal or lamb, or for vegetables, rissoles or savoury puddings. Use it too in dumplings or forcemeat balls in stews, and especially for rabbit stew or vegetable casserole. Try a pinch in batter puddings or savoury pancakes for a change.

Lemon thyme has a distinct lemon flavour and it can be used in the same way as black thyme. Both varieties are easy to grow and they take up very little room. A pot of each will be enough to last for the season.

TARRAGON

This is mostly used to flavour vinegar for sauces and salad dressings, etc. Steep a cupful of Tarragon leaves in two pints of wine vinegar for about six weeks, then strain off and bottle. Add a little Tarragon vinegar to mayonnaise, to the making of mustard or for the gravy of braised beef or rabbit or vegetables. Finely chopped Tarragon leaves are delicious in a casserole of rabbit or chicken.

CHERVIL

This herb can be used as a substitute for parsley and it goes particularly well with eggs or fish.

A mixture of chervil, tarragon, parsley and chives gives a distinctive flavour to omelets, other egg dishes, and salads. Just chop them finely and sprinkle over at the last moment.

Use marjoram, basil and sage in the same way.

CHIVES

The green part of chives chopped up in salads, soups or sandwiches tastes just like spring onion. A large clump of chives grown in a window-box will supply all the onion flavouring that you need.

SAGE

Sage is good with lamb or with casserole of vegetables. In fact, vegetable dishes with sage and chives for flavouring taste so good that you scarcely miss the meat. Well-made vegetable cutlets or pasties need a little sage to make them more interesting.

MINT

Remember that you can use freshly chopped mint in dumplings or in a summer vegetable stew, or in pasties filled with new carrots and green peas.

Use it, too, in sandwiches with home-made "sour-milk" cheese. Make mint jelly, sometimes, to serve with curries instead of chutneys. Sprinkle mint in a green-pea soup ; add it to a puree made from home-dried peas or to a soup in which young green pea pods have been used.

See page 107, SOUP.

A hot salad of young vegetables, such as turnips, carrots, peas, and potatoes with a mint-flavoured white sauce is delicious.

You can make it even more summery by adding a little diced cucumber to the salad.

Mint tea is refreshing and very simply made. Pour boiling water over a handful of bruised mint leaves in a basin, allow to infuse thoroughly and place it on a cool shelf or in the refrigerator to chill. Iced tea with mint flavouring is a Canadian drink for summer.

DILL

This herb is very little used, but it is easy to grow from seed. It can be used for flavouring soup or sauce. It is good, too, sprinkled on grilled fish, especially the oily kind such as the herring.

Try serving dill sauce instead of caper sauce with boiled mutton.

HORSERADISH

Horseradish sauce is an excellent flavour for soused or grilled herrings and for grilled white fish. Horseradish is a good source of Vitamin C. Horseradish combines well with any beetroot dish.

Grated horseradish mixed with stewed apple is good, too, and can be served with any meat dish.

The secret of clever flavouring is to be imaginative but sparing. Overdoing the flavouring is almost as bad as having none at all. Experiment every day with new flavours or fresh combinations of them, so that your cooking never becomes dull. When fresh herbs are plentiful, is the time to dry off a good supply and bottle them for the winter.

HERB PUDDING (to serve with Meat)

To Eleanor Sinclair Rhode, from her *Culinary and Salad Herbs*, we are indebted for the following recipe.

" This is a well-known Westmorland recipe, and is there called Easter Pudding, because one of the chief ingredients is Polygonum bistorta, popularly known as Easter May Giant or Easter Ledges. . . . This native herb is not a necessary ingredient, and the pudding can be made at any time of year and is most useful for making meat go farther.

To a pint of cooked barley, allow two heaping table-spoons of finely chopped herbs and leaves that are at their best in spring—young blackcurrant leaves, Easter May Giant, parsley, mint, dandelion, etc., together with an eggspoonful of finely chopped onion. Add the mixture with seasoning, and a beaten egg, to the barley and bake in a greased pudding dish. The addition of a little butter or margarine is advisable if rations will run to it."

Failing margarine, of course, clarified dripping could be used. In winter-time, when there are few fresh herbs available, dried herbs could be included.

PICKLED NASTURTIUM SEEDS

For use in place of Capers.

Choose matured but not too large seeds for the best flavour. To each pint of vinegar allow 5-6 peppercorns and ½ oz. of salt. A bay leaf gives added flavour.

Boil the vinegar, salt, bay leaf and the peppercorns together, then cover and draw the pan aside and allow them to infuse for about 30 minutes on the back of the stove. Use hot or cool down, and strain off the pickling vinegar ready for use.

Pick the seeds on a dry day, wash them in cold water, and place them in a bowl. Pour over a brine made from dissolving half a teacup of salt in a pint of water, and allow to stand for some hours. Rinse well, place the seeds in hot sterilised bottles or jars, pour on boiling vinegar to cover and seal down while hot.

FISH

FISH is a Body-building Food; oily fish like herrings, sprats, mackerel and salmon are Protective Foods also.

We can give fish to children, to invalids, to men doing long hours of heavy work. It contains as much nourishment as meat.

We do not always make fish dishes as interesting as we might. We should lose the idea that potatoes are their only possible accompaniment and remember to serve them with salads or green vegetables as well.

HERRINGS are one of the best of all foods. They are full of nourishment, and rich in qualities that build up the body and protect it from illness. They are invaluable for growing children, and can be served at any meal, breakfast, lunch, tea or supper.

How to Bone a Herring.—Most people find this method of boning is the easiest. If you do not possess a sharp knife, use a pair of kitchen scissors. First, cut off the head of the fish, clean and scale. Then cut open along the belly. Open out the fish and carefully loosen the small bones on each side of the backbone with your thumb and forefinger and pull it steadily away from the flesh. You will find that the small bones will come away with the backbone.

How to Treat the Roes.—When the roes are removed, handle them as little as possible. Put them on a plate, dividing the hard from the soft. They can be cooked and served with the herrings, or, if you prefer, will make a dish by themselves.

How to Open a Herring when Cooked.—Plump up the herring with the knife and fork. Slit down the centre of the back from head to tail, inserting the knife just far enough to touch the backbone. Gently lay back the flesh on the side uppermost, thus revealing the backbone with the smaller bones attached to it. Now insert the knife under the backbone and strip it out gently. It will come clean away.

Do not think that because a herring has no roe, it is not in prime condition. A young herring is always without roe.

BOILED HERRINGS

Behead, clean and scale the fish. Cook for a couple of minutes in rapidly boiling water which has been heavily salted (about a handful of salt to half a pint of water). The brine prevents the goodness from boiling out of the fish. Remove, strain and serve at once, with parsley sauce. Or, serve cold with salad.

DRY FRYING—FRYING IN SALT

There is so much oil in the flesh of a herring that it is quite possible to fry it without any other fat if you have a strong, iron frying pan. Do not try this method with a thin pan or it will burn.

Sprinkle the pan with salt, heat gently at first, shaking occasionally. Continue heating until the pan is almost red-hot, then lay in the herrings, which must be scaled, cleaned, washed and dried. Fry on each side until golden brown and crisp—3 to 4 minutes each side. Serve piping hot.

FRYING IN SHALLOW FAT

In this method a very small amount of fat is put in the pan. Two teaspoons of frying fat will be sufficient for three or four herrings. Make the fat hot in your pan before putting in the fish. Then continue as in the recipe above.

FRYING IN OATMEAL

4 medium-sized fish.	½ teaspoon salt.
2 tablespoons fine oatmeal.	A very little frying fat.

Clean the herrings and remove heads, tails and fins. Wipe with damp cloth. Have the fine oatmeal and salt shaken together in paper. Coat each herring with the dry mixture, put at once into the hot fat and fry for five minutes. Turn the fish carefully with a slice and fry the other side a golden brown. Serve on hot plates with a sprinkle of vinegar if liked. (This serves 4 people.)

BAKED HERRINGS

6 herrings.	½ teaspoon of margarine.
Salt and pepper.	2 oz. breadcrumbs—if liked.

Cut off heads and tails, scale and clean the fish. Grease a baking dish, lay in the fish, sprinkle with the breadcrumbs, pepper and salt. Cover with a piece of greaseproof paper and bake in a moderate oven for about 10 minutes. Then remove the paper and leave the fish in the oven for another 5 minutes to brown. You will find that there is practically no smell during cooking by this method. If you do not want to heat the oven, cook the fish in a covered casserole on top of the stove or over a gas jet low enough not to touch the pot. (This serves 6 people.)

BAKED STUFFED HERRINGS

4 herrings.	1 large soft roe or 2 hard roes.
6 tablespoons of breadcrumbs.	1 small onion.
1 teaspoon chopped parsley or ½ teaspoon mixed herbs.	½ teaspoon margarine or cooking fat.

Pepper and salt.

Remove heads, clean and wash fish. Split open and remove the backbones.

To make stuffing, mix the breadcrumbs, roe, herbs, parsley and seasoning. You will find that the roe will bind the mixture. Mix well. Then sprinkle the inside of each herring with pepper and salt and spread on a portion of the stuffing. Roll up and keep in place by tying with coarse white cotton or piercing with a small wooden skewer. To cook, grease a pie-dish, lay in the fish, cover with a lid or greaseproof paper. Bake for 15 minutes, then remove lid or paper and allow to brown. If preferred, instead of rolling up the fish, spread the insides with the stuffing, fold the fish back into shape and bake as before.

Potatoes baked in their jackets and hot baked beetroot (served with vinaigrette sauce) may be cooked at the same time, and, with the herrings, will provide a delicious, economical meal. (This serves 4 people.)

SOUSED HERRINGS

6 or 8 herrings.	1 breakfastcup water.
1 tablespoon mixed pickling spice.	1 level teaspoon salt.
	1 onion if possible.

Cut off the heads and tails, clean and bone the fish. Roll up with a slice of onion inside each fish. Pack in a baking dish (not baking tin). Scatter pickling spice between the rolls, add remainder of onion sliced. Sprinkle in salt, pour in vinegar and water, mixed together. Bay leaves may be added if liked. Bake in a slow oven for one and a half hours. If preferred, do not bone fish but lay in dish, alternately thick end to thin end.

Different districts have their own traditional methods of preparing soused herrings. A small piece of bruised root ginger, half a dozen stalks (stems only) of parsley, fresh shallots, and even chunks of cucumber may be added to the baking dish.

GRILLED HERRINGS

2 herrings. | 1 tablespoon chopped parsley.
Mustard sauce.

Scale and clean the fish, then wipe with a clean cloth.
Upon each side of the herrings make three cuts 1½ inches
apart, cutting down to, not through, the backbone. Remove the heads. Grill quickly under a very hot grill till
brown on each side. Dust lightly with salt, sprinkle with
chopped parsley, and serve with mustard sauce. (See
page 115, SAUCES.)

HERRINGS IN JELLY

Bone, roll, season and bake four fresh herrings. Allow
to get quite cold. Cover 3d. worth of fish bones with
water to which you have added pepper and salt and a
flavouring of herbs and spices, as liked. Simmer for a
couple of hours ; you will be surprised at the amount of
gelatinous matter that comes from them. Pour this jelly-
like substance into a bowl, put in the herring rolls and
allow to set. Turn out and serve with green salad. If
obtainable, a packet of aspic jelly may be dissolved and
used instead of simmering the bones.

HERRING ROES—SOFT ROES

Simmer them in a little milk for 10 minutes. Drain
carefully. Curl the roes and place on toast with a tiny
sprig of parsley on each.

SOFT ROE POTATO CAKES

Simmer the roes for 5 minutes, then mash with at least
twice the quantity of cooked potatoes, season with pepper
and salt, shape into cakes, and fry as fish cakes in a very
little hot fat.

SOFT ROES FOR CHILDREN

Children over a year old may be given a small portion
of soft roe cooked in milk. Mash the roe with a little
baked potato, creamed spinach or other vegetable.
Begin with a teaspoon of roe and increase it gradually
to a tablespoon. The roe, being rich in Vitamin A, is a
substitute for cod liver oil.

POACHED KIPPERS

When cooking kippers for children try poaching them ;
the meat comes away from the bones easily when cooked

like this. Cut off heads, put fish in frying pan with just enough water to cover. Bring to the boil and simmer for a few minutes. Drain well and serve with a sprinkling of parsley on each.

" JUGGED " KIPPER

A simple way of poaching a kipper is to curl it up and place it in a jug. Pour on enough boiling water to cover, and stand for 5 minutes in a warm place. Strain and serve as above.

GRILLED KIPPER

I slice of toast	Small amount of margarine or
Dash of pepper and vinegar.	dripping for each kipper.

Heat the grill ; make the toast, then lay it on the grill under the grid. Wipe each kipper with a damp cloth and behead. Lay on hot grid skin side uppermost and grill for a minute. Then turn the fish and on the fleshy side lay a nut of fat. Cook for 5 or 6 minutes. Serve each kipper on a slice of toast with a tiny pinch of pepper over, and, if liked, a dash of vinegar.

GRILLED BLOATERS

Allow I bloater for each person.
A little margarine or dripping for frying the roes.

Heat the grill and grease the grid with a little margarine or dripping before placing the fish on it. When one side is brown, turn over and grill backs and serve with a sprinkling of spiced vinegar, if liked.

FILLETED BLOATERS ON BAKED BREAD

Allow I bloater for each person.	Pinch of pepper and a round of
A dash of vinegar.	wheatmeal bread for each.

Split open the fish and remove the flesh from the bones in long fillets. Place bread on greased baking tin or fire-proof dish. Lay on the fillets, season them with pepper and a sprinkling of vinegar. Bake in a brisk oven for about 8 minutes and serve very hot.

BLOATERS FOR LUNCH

When you have filleted bloaters for a special supper or breakfast dish, grill a few more fillets than are required for the actual meal. While still very hot lay these extra ones between spread slices of bread. Allow these to get cold, then pack them as lunch-time sandwiches.

Cold grilled fillets, with a few spring onions or freshly

sliced tomatoes from the garden, make a good summer snack. Add a few crisp lettuce leaves to the dish.

WHITE FISH

When you have your fish filleted by a fishmonger always ask for the trimmings and bones. Put these in a saucepan in water or milk and water to cover. Add a few broken parsley stalks, a small piece of onion if possible, and a few peppercorns. Simmer for half an hour and then strain off the liquor. This will give you a good fish stock which you can use to make soup or sauce and in which you can cook fish. You should use this at once as it does not keep.

Do not soak fish long in water when you are washing it. It is best to wash fish quickly under running water from a tap to avoid delay and then rinse quickly in cold water in a basin.

Fish can be steamed, boiled, baked, stewed, fried, grilled or poached. Thin slices of fish should not be boiled, but poached.

To poach fish, take a clean baking tin or a shallow saucepan; grease it and lay in the fish; season with salt and pepper, barely cover with fish stock, then lay over a piece of greased paper and cook the fish in the oven or on top of the stove very gently until the flesh is done. This will take only 10 minutes or so, if the pieces are small. Use the liquid to make sauce.

Steamed fish is very good, very digestible and particularly suitable for invalids. If you have no steamer, wash and dry the fish; put it on a greased plate; dot with light flakes of margarine, cover with a saucepan lid and stand the plate on top of a saucepan of boiling water to cook until the fish is tender. Thin pieces of fish take about 15 minutes this way.

CASSEROLE OF FISH

1½ lb. of any white fish cut into convenient pieces.	Dessertspoon of chopped parsley.
1 oz. of dripping or margarine.	Pepper and salt.
1 lb. potatoes.	½ pint fish stock.
1 teacup milk.	1½ oz. flour.
3-4 carrots.	Pinch of mixed herbs.

Cut the fish into convenient pieces. Melt the fat in a casserole and add the carrots finely sliced. Fry very lightly for a few minutes, then stir in the flour. Next add the stock gradually, stirring all the time, and last of all the milk. Add herbs, salt and pepper to taste, and allow the sauce to cook for about 3 minutes. Add the fish and the potatoes cut in slices. Replace the lid on the casserole and simmer very gently in the oven for 30 to 40 minutes. On no account allow the mixture to boil. Serve hot with a sprinkling of finely chopped parsley.

CASSEROLE OF FISH WITH GARDEN HERBS

1½ lb. of any white fish cut into convenient pieces.	1 bayleaf or few leaves of tarragon or fennel.
2-3 carrots.	1 pint of fish stock or 1 pint of milk and water (half in half).
4 potatoes.	
Salt, pepper.	

2 artichokes or 2 sticks of celery.

Prepare and slice the vegetables ; place in a casserole together with the fish. Pour over the hot stock, season lightly with salt and pepper and put on lid. Simmer gently for about 1 hour and remove the herbs just before serving.

FISH CAKES

½ lb. cooked white fish.	Frying fat (optional).
1 lb. mashed potatoes.	Little fine oatmeal or flour.
1 dessertspoon chopped parsley.	Pepper and salt.

Take away all bones and skin from fish. Mash fish with fork and mix with the mashed potatoes and chopped parsley. Season with salt and pepper. Bind the mixture with a little milk. Divide into required number of cakes—two to each person. Dust with flour or oatmeal and roll into required shape with hands. Fry a golden brown in a very little smoking fat. Or bake in the oven.

CHINESE FISH DISH

1½ lb. cod or other round white fish.	1 teaspoon Worcester sauce.
	Few spring onions if possible.
2-3 tablespoons frying oil.	1 dessertspoon cornflour.
A little chopped bacon.	½ pint water.
2-3 oz. mushroom stalks.	Seasoning.

Wash and scale the fish and cut into thin cutlets. Slice the bacon and the spring onion. Heat the oil in a saucepan and fry the bacon and onion till lightly brown. Add the fish and fry for 2 or 3 minutes. Add water, chopped mushroom stalks and Worcester sauce. Simmer for about 25 minutes and thicken with the cornflour slaked in a little cold water. Bring to boil, add seasoning and turn out very carefully. (This serves 4 people.)

CRUMBED COD STEAKS

4 cod steaks.	4 oz. brown breadcrumbs.
I oz. dripping.	A good pinch of mixed herbs,
2-3 tablespoons milk.	Salt and pepper.

Wash the steaks and brush with milk. Toss carefully in breadcrumbs previously seasoned with salt, herbs and pepper. Place the fish in a greased baking dish, dot with the rest of the dripping and bake for 25 to 30 minutes in a moderate oven. Garnish with parsley.

CURRIED MACKEREL

Any firm, solid fish can be curried. Prawns, cod, hake, halibut and haddock are all suitable. Mackerel is particularly nice.

1½ lb. mackerel (or other fish).	I small tablespoon curry powder.
I oz. margarine or other fat.	½ bunch spring onions.
I tablespoon chutney or sweet pickle (home-made).	½ pint water.
	I dessertspoon flour. Salt.

Remove heads, trim fish and wash well, scraping the inside out very thoroughly. Cut the fish into convenient pieces and sprinkle with salt. Dice the onions. Fry the curry powder and flour gently in fat for at least 10 minutes (much of the success of the curry depends on this slow preliminary frying), add the onions, and fry till they are just turning colour, and then stir in the water. Bring to boil and place fish and chutney in it. Simmer gently for half an hour, add the seasoning and serve accompanied by mashed potatoes.

SCALLOPS OF FISH

Try these for supper—

½ lb. cooked fish.	I lb. left-over mashed potatoes.
Left-over sauce or a little white or parsley sauce.	I oz. dripping.
	2 oz. breadcrumbs.

Flake the fish and mix with sauce and potato. Put in scallop shells, sprinkle with breadcrumbs, dot over with flakes of dripping and bake until heated right through. A slice of cooked tomato makes a nice finish and looks tempting. (This serves 4 people.)

FRESH WATER FISH

The Fresh Water Fish in our rivers are home-grown produce. Here are a few recipes for cooking the most usual kinds.

GRILLED BREAM
2 lb. fish.

First soak the fish, seasoned with salt and pepper, in a mixture of 4 tablespoons of oil, 2 tablespoons of vinegar, a few diced spring onions, a few chopped parsley stalks, thyme and half a bay leaf broken into little pieces. Leave the fish in this for an hour, having first scored it on each side with cuts about a quarter of an inch deep and three-quarters of an inch apart, turning once or twice. When you are ready to cook it, remove any bits of herbs, brush it over well with the marinade and grill it on each side. (This serves 4 or 5 people.)

BAKED ROACH

Open the roach down the back, remove the backbone and season with salt, pepper and mixed herbs. Flour the fish and then coat with a thin batter of flour and water, and then breadcrumbs ; put them into a greased fireproof dish, sprinkle with chopped parsley and thyme, and bake in the oven for a quarter of an hour.

SALMON TROUT

Poach in a very little boiling salty water and serve with melted margarine.

GRILLED TROUT

Make three gashes on each side of the trout, roll them gently in a little oil seasoned with salt and pepper, and grill them gently, 4 minutes on each side.

Almost any kind of fish makes a good salad. Cook it, and when cold, flake it and lay it on lettuce leaves, or make it the centre of a mixed vegetable salad. Dress it with home-made mayonnaise, with French dressing or cold sauce.

MEAT
Using Cheaper Cuts of Meat

MANY young housewives find shopping at the butcher's difficult because they do not know the names of the cheaper cuts of meat, nor how best to serve them. In this chapter we are aiming to show you that, weight for weight, they present the same food value and acceptability as the more expensive kinds, if you are ready to take a little care in making up the recipes.

Here is a list of the cheaper cuts of meat that are suitable for stewing and braising :—

CHEAPER CUTS FOR STEWING AND BRAISING.

Beef.—Fresh brisket ; leg or shin ; flank, chuck steak ; ox cheek ; neck, also called clod or sticking piece ; oxtail ; cow-heel ; tripe ; ox heart.

Mutton.—Neck ; breast ; sheep's head ; trotters ; heart.

Veal.—Neck ; breast ; knuckle ; veal pieces.

CHEAPER CUTS FOR BOILING.

Beef.—Fresh silverside ; flank (very economical) ; brisket ; salt aitch-bone (cheap, but contains a lot of bone) ; salt silverside ; salt brisket ; salt thin end of flank ; salt neck, called clod sticking.

Pork.—Hand with foot (often called " fat hen " : is usually boiled but can be roasted) ; spring or belly (usually served cold) ; neck and shoulder ; pig's head ; trotters ; pickled pork.

CHEAPER CUTS FOR SLOW ROASTING.

Beef.—Best end of flank ; fresh aitchbone (see above) ; thin flank, rolled and boneless ; back ribs ; top ribs ; brisket, boneless.

Mutton.—Breast (usually boned, stuffed, and rolled for roasting : use bones for soup) ; best end of neck.

Pork.—Hand with foot (" fat hen ").

Veal.—Breast (see above for mutton) ; best end of neck.

MAIN RULES IN COOKING MEAT

Your chief aims when cooking meat are its tenderness and the preservation of its essential goodness. No matter whether you are grilling, roasting, boiling or stewing it, always cook the meat as quickly as you can for the first few minutes. This seals in the juices.

To boil meat.—Have the stock or water actually at

boiling point when the joint is lowered into it. Allow the pan to boil fast for 3-5 minutes, then reduce the heat and simmer for the remaining period of cooking.

To roast meat.—Place it first in a very hot oven to seal the meat, then reduce the temperature after 15 minutes to a moderate heat.

To stew meat.—Tender meat can be fried for a few minutes to seal in the juices. Tough meat should be put into stock or gravy at the simmer.

To grill meat.—Have the grill very hot before you start. Grill on one side at full heat, then turn the food over and cook the other side for two minutes. Finish cooking on both sides at lower heat.

TIME FOR COOKING MEAT.

For roasting beef.—Allow 15 minutes to the lb. and 15 minutes over for the whole joint.

For roasting mutton.—Allow 15-20 minutes to the lb. and 20 minutes over.

For roasting pork or veal.—Allow 25 minutes to the lb. and 25 minutes over.

For roasting stuffed meats.—Allow 25 minutes to the lb. and 25 minutes over on the joint.

A large joint takes relatively less time in comparison with a small one, by poundage. A joint which is boned, stuffed or rolled takes a little longer and, whatever the meat, must be calculated at the higher rate for the cooking.

Cook cheaper cuts of meat as often as possible in casserole, always with the lid on. This method of cooking, in a limited quantity of liquid, makes them succulent and well flavoured. It also saves you both trouble and fuel, as vegetables are cooked in with the meat, and a minimum of heat is sufficient to keep the pot gently cooking.

BRAISED BRISKET OF BEEF

About 3 lb. fresh brisket.	1 oz. dripping.
2 lb. mixed vegetables (carrots, parsnips, turnip, celery, etc.).	A pinch of mixed herbs (if liked). Salt and pepper. Stock or water. 1 oz. flour.

Season the flour with salt and pepper and dust the meat with it. Make the fat very hot in a pan. Put in the meat and brown each side. Take out the meat, put in the sliced vegetables and toss them in the saucepan for a few minutes—take out half of them, then put back the meat and cover with the rest of the vegetables ; add herbs and seasoning. Put on the lid, then add enough boiling water or stock to come half-way up the meat.

Cook very slowly, on top of the stove, or in the oven for at least 2½ hours.

BEEF IN CASSEROLE

1½ lb. of stewing beef.	1 stick of celery (if you have it).
2 large carrots.	½ bay leaf (if you like).
1 turnip.	A small pinch of mixed herbs.
1 onion or 2 leeks, if possible.	1 small teaspoon of mixed spice.

Stock, vegetable water or water.

Cut up the beef into 2-inch cubes, toss in a very little hot fat in a pan, and brown it on all sides, turning it over after a minute. Cut up the vegetables and put a layer in the casserole. Lay the browned meat on top and cover with the vegetables, adding the herbs, bay leaf and spice, any of which you can leave out. Season with pepper and salt and pour in about ¾ pint of hot stock or water from cooked vegetables or potatoes or plain water. If the lid does not fit quite tightly, cover the pot with greased paper before putting on the lid. Cook gently in a slow oven or over a low burner until the meat is tender (at least 2 hours). Take out the bunch of herbs and serve from the casserole.

JUGGED BEEF[1]

2 lb. of leg or shin of beef.	¾ pint of water.
6 cloves.	1 onion, if possible.
Several outside leaves of cab-bage.	5-6 carrots.
	A little cayenne pepper and salt.

Cut the beef into 2-inch cubes, put in a deep pan, add the water, pepper and salt. Stick the cloves into the onion and put in the pan with the sliced carrots and finely shredded cabbage. Bring to the boil. After 10 minutes of steady cooking wrap the pan in newspaper and put immediately into the hay-box. Put on the hay cushion and fasten down the lid of the box and leave for 4 to 5 hours.

OATMEAL MINCE

1 lb. skirt of beef.	Salt, pepper.
2 grated carrots (large).	4 oz. toasted oatmeal (coarse).

Vegetable stock or water.

Have ready the coarse oatmeal freshly toasted, and work it into the prepared and minced beef, with good seasonings of salt and pepper and the grated carrot. Moisten with vegetable boilings or a little water and cook in a covered casserole for 2½-3 hours, either in the

[1] For Hay-Box Cooking, see p. 123.

oven or, with a little more liquid, on the top of the range.
(Sufficient for 4 people.)

SALT BEEF AND DUMPLINGS

3 lb. salt silverside (or salt aitchbone or salt brisket).	I small turnip.
	I onion, if possible.
5-6 carrots. I parsnip.	A few peppercorns.

For the Dumplings, see p. 97, OATMEAL.

Always ask your butcher how long the meat has been
in its salt brine. If it is heavily salted, soak it for a few
hours in cold water. Then tie it into a neat round with
string and put it in a pan with enough water to cover
the meat entirely, bring it *very slowly* to the boil and skim
well. Simmer for 1 hour and skim again. Next add the
vegetables, sliced, with peppercorns and simmer for 15
minutes. Lastly, put in the dumplings and simmer for a
further 15 minutes.

To make the dumplings, mix the dry ingredients
together and bind with a little milk or water. The dough
must be soft but not sticky. With floured hands, make it
into balls.

To serve, put meat on hot dish, with dumplings and
vegetables round it.

NOTE.—Stewing mutton may be cooked in exactly the
same way.

MINCED MEAT ROLY

I lb. raw minced beef.	½ lb. grated raw carrots.
3 oz. suet.	Swede or parsnip.
1½ teaspoons baking powder.	I onion, if possible.
2 oz. grated raw potato.	¾ lb. flour.
Pepper and salt.	

Moisten meat and vegetables together and season with
salt and pepper. Make pastry with flour, potato, suet,
baking powder and water to mix. Roll out on floured
board and spread meat and vegetables on it. Leave a
margin of half an inch all round and moisten this with
water. Roll up and press edges together firmly. Roll in
margarine papers or floured cloth and steam for about
2½ hours.

BAKE-HOUSE MUTTON

2 breasts of lamb (boned).	½ lb. onions or leeks, if possible.
2½-3 lb. potatoes.	I teacup water.
Salt and pepper.	

Scrub the potatoes and cut into thick slices. Peel and

slice the onions. Put a good layer of potatoes in a baking tin, then the onions, if you have them, and add the rest of the potatoes, seasoning each layer with salt and pepper. Pour on the water.

Roll up the breasts, lay on top of the potatoes, cover with margarine papers and bake in a moderate oven for $1\frac{1}{2}$ hours. Remove paper and brown the meat for about 20 minutes before serving.

(Enough for 4-5 people.)

SPRING BRAISE

3 lb. scrag end neck of lamb or mutton. Seasoning.	2 lb. cabbage or spring greens. Several peppercorns.

Wash the meat and put in a large saucepan with just enough water to cover, and a little salt and the peppercorns. Bring to the boil and simmer as slowly as you can for at least $1\frac{1}{2}$ hours. Slice the greens finely and add to the pan ; cover and cook for another ten minutes. Serve with the liquid in the pan, which may be thickened with gravy powder if preferred.

MEAT ROLL

1 lb. lean mutton. [meat.	1 lb. skirt of beef.
2 oz. bacon pieces or sausage	2 breakfastcups breadcrumbs.
$\frac{1}{4}$ teaspoon mixed herbs.	2 tablespoons chopped pickles (if liked).
Salt, pepper.	
A little milk.	$\frac{1}{2}$ teaspoon mixed spice.

Mince the meat and bacon, mix well with all the dry ingredients and the pickles, putting a few breadcrumbs on one side. Bind with a little milk.

Put into a greased and crumb-coated cake tin and bake in a brisk oven for about 45 minutes. Serve hot or cold.

(Enough for two meals—4-5 people.)

CHINA CHILOE

A Recipe for Gardeners.

About 2 lb. breast of lamb—sticking.	$\frac{1}{2}$ pint shelled peas.
	2 onions.
$\frac{1}{2}$ cucumber.	2 oz. dripping.
2 lettuces.	Pepper and salt.

Stew the meat slowly in a little water until cooked. Then remove bones and skin and mince the meat.

Slice the cucumbers, onions and lettuces. Melt 2 oz. dripping in a casserole or pan. Put in the vegetables, season with salt and pepper and cook slowly for 10 minutes. Then add the minced meat and a teacup of the water in which the meat was boiled. Simmer for another 20 minutes. Serve with a border of mashed potatoes.

LAMB WITH CELERY

1 lb. boned breast of lamb, finely diced.	2 tablespoons fine oatmeal or flour.
1 lb. potatoes.	2 tablespoons margarine.
2 cups chopped celery.	Trimmings of lamb fat.
2 dessertspoons chopped celery foliage.	1 teaspoon salt.
	Pepper to taste.

Melt the trimmed lamb fat in a shallow pan, then add the lamb. Cook, stirring frequently until light brown. Add potatoes, scrubbed and sliced, the celery and celery foliage, and cook very gently for 1 hour in the oven or on top of the stove, adding ½ pint of vegetable water or water.

Blend the flour with a little cold vegetable water to a thick cream, add a little boiling stock to it, then return all to the saucepan and simmer until evenly thickened. Season with salt and pepper to taste and serve hot. Be sure to save the bones from the breast for soup.

(Enough for 4-6 people.)

STUFFED LAMB

3 lb. breast of lamb.	Potato and watercress stuffing, see below.

One way to serve a breast of lamb is to bone, stuff and either roast or braise it. To bone the breast—take a sharp knife, score round the bones and work the flesh away from them—lifting them away cleanly. Trim away surplus fat.

Spread the boned breasts with the stuffing—roll up and tie firmly. Put in baking pan with a teacup of water. Roast very slowly for 1¼ hours, basting every 20 minutes. Potatoes or other vegetables can be baked round the joint.

FOR THE STUFFING

1 lb. hot potatoes.	2 tablespoons milk.
1 oz. margarine or dripping.	1 bunch watercress, well washed and chopped.
1 teaspoon mixed herbs.	

Salt and pepper.

Mix together, beat in enough milk to bind (about 2 tablespoons—hot), and your stuffing is ready.

MUTTON WITH TURNIPS

1½ to 2 lb. neck of mutton.
2 lb. turnips.
1 tablespoon chopped parsley.

1 breakfastcup stock or hot water.
1 dessertspoon flour.

Salt and pepper.

Cut meat in neat pieces. Remove surplus fat and chop finely, then frizzle down in a pan or casserole. Peel and slice the turnips and fry in the fat until golden brown. A sprinkling of sugar, if you can spare it, is an improvement. Then remove the turnips, put in the meat dusted with the flour and brown. Pour in the hot stock or water, add pepper and salt and the onion, chopped, and stew very slowly, covered, in the oven or on top of the stove, for at least 1 hour. Then add the turnips and cook for another ½ hour. Sprinkle over chopped parsley before serving.

VEAL WITH RICE

2 lb. knuckle or breast of veal.
½ lb. rice.

1 large head of celery.
1 tablespoon chopped parsley.

Salt and pepper.

Put the meat in a saucepan with enough hot water to cover. Bring to the boil very slowly and skim well. Add the celery, washed and cut in small pieces, and the salt and pepper. Stew very slowly for 1 hour. Then add the rice and cook for another hour. Just before serving add the chopped parsley.

RABBITS

If you want to tell the age of a rabbit, take its head in your hand and squeeze it. If it gives easily, the rabbit is a young one. If it feels hard, it means that the rabbit is better for stewing than for frying or baking. If it has long protruding teeth, then it is too old to eat at all. It is worth while to look at the kidneys. If they are surrounded with clear, firm fat, it is a good healthy rabbit.

BAKED RABBIT

With Dried-plum Forcemeat

1 rabbit.
½ lb. dried plums.
1 tablespoon flour.
Salt, pepper.
1 oz. dripping or margarine.
Fat for frying.

1 teacup wheatmeal breadcrumbs. [oatmeal.
1 teacup of toasted medium
1 tablespoon chopped parsley.
Milk to bind.
Salt, pepper.

Soak the fruit overnight, then stone it. Soak the rabbit in lukewarm water for half an hour. Dry. Cut into joints and cover them with flour, seasoned with pepper and salt. Shake to leave them coated in flour, and fry in a little very hot fat till brown.

Simmer the head, neck, liver and heart in water to make gravy. Pack the joints in a baking dish and add forcemeat balls, made as follows :

Mix together the wheatmeal crumbs and the toasted oatmeal, add good seasoning of pepper and salt and the chopped parsley, then bind to a stiff consistency with a little milk.

Roll each of the stoned fruits in this mixture. Pack them between the joints in the baking dish, add the gravy from the head, etc., and bake for one hour.

BOILED RABBIT

1 rabbit.	2 lb. mixed root vegetables.
1 oz. suet.	1 oz. flour.
4 oz. breadcrumbs.	1 oz. margarine.
Parsley—1 bunch.	$\frac{1}{2}$ pint milk.
Mixed herbs.	Seasoning. Salt and pepper.

Soak the rabbit in warm salt water. Remove all internal organs, putting the liver on one side. Simmer the heart, kidneys, lungs, etc., in a little salt water to make a gravy. Chop the suet and mix together with the crumbs, salt and pepper, 1 tablespoon parsley and mixed herbs. Add the finely chopped liver, bind with a little beaten egg or milk. Put this stuffing inside the rabbit and sew it up. Truss the rabbit by drawing the front legs towards the back and fastening the back legs over them. Fasten with small skewers and string.

Boil the rabbit gently for $1\frac{1}{2}$ hours in just enough water to cover. Half an hour before it is ready, add the prepared vegetables cut into neat pieces. Meanwhile, prepare $\frac{1}{2}$ pint parsley sauce to coat the rabbit.

To do this melt the margarine, stir in the flour and cook together for a few minutes. Then add the milk slowly and bring to the boil, stirring all the time. Then add 1 teacup of the boilings from the heart, etc., and two dessertspoons of finely chopped parsley. Season with salt and pepper and simmer at least for 3 minutes.

Remove the rabbit, untie the string and take out the skewers, arranging rabbit on hot dish. Coat with the parsley sauce and serve with the mixed vegetables. Garnish with light sprigs of parsley.

Use the liquid in the saucepan as described in the next recipe.

RABBIT DUMPLINGS

2-3 fleshy joints cooked rabbit, also broth in which they were cooked (see above).

Scraps of bacon, if possible.
8 oz. self-raising flour.
2 oz. chopped suet.

Water to mix.

Remove the meat from the joint and chop finely. Sieve the flour into a basin, add a pinch of salt and the finely chopped suet, then the prepared meat with finely chopped bacon if this is to be used. Mix with a little water to a stiff paste and form into small dumplings with floured fingers. Boil these in the broth in which the rabbit was cooked with the lid on the pan, and serve broth and dumplings together.

CURRIED RABBIT

1 rabbit.
1 dessertspoon curry powder.
1 dessertspoon flour.
1 apple.
6 diced spring onions.

Salt and pepper.
1 oz. dripping.
½ pint stock or water.
1 pinch sugar.
Vinegar to sharpen.

Wash and dry the rabbit and cut into neat joints. Roll these in flour, seasoned with salt and pepper, and dry quickly in the hot fat until lightly brown. Remove the rabbit. Grate the apple and chop the spring onions. Stir lightly, adding curry powder. Stir well until the ingredients are all a rich brown colour, then add the stock and bring to the boil. Replace the joints and simmer gently for one and a half hours. Add a dash of vinegar to sharpen and a pinch of sugar before serving.

JUGGED RABBIT

1 rabbit.
Small pieces of fat bacon, if possible.
A few spring onions.
3-4 carrots.
1 oz. pearl barley.

6 cloves.
Small bunch mixed herbs.
1 bay leaf.
Cayenne and alt to taste.
¾ pint hot water.
1 dessertspoon flour.

Joint the rabbit and rub in flour previously seasoned with salt and pepper. Put in stewjar with the bacon, barley, cloves, sliced carrots, and tie herbs and bay leaf in a muslin bag. Place in the stewjar with hot water, salt and pepper and put into a hot oven. Turn the heat down as low as possible. Cook gently for 3 hours. Before serving remove the bag of herbs. Redcurrant jelly is a good relish with this dish if you have it, and a few force-meat balls may be served with it if liked.

POTTED RABBIT

4 oz. cooked rabbit.	1 oz. margarine.
A pinch each of allspice and nutmeg.	Salt and pepper.
	Mutton fat to seal.

Remove the bone and skin from the meat, then pass twice through the mincer. Melt the margarine and add it to the meat with seasonings, pinch of pepper, allspice and nutmeg. Pound well together and press the meat tightly into small pots or glasses, then pour a little melted mutton fat over the top to seal. This makes a nourishing spread for carried lunch.

CURRIED VENISON

Cut 1 lb. lean venison into 2-inch cubes. Season with salt and pepper. Fry with an onion, an apple or a tomato, and add a dessertspoon of curry powder and a pinch of ginger. Add a breakfastcup of stock and cook slowly for two or three hours with the lid on the pan, stirring occasionally, and add more stock, as required. Ten minutes before serving stir in a tablespoon of chutney or sweet pickle and a pinch of sugar.

IRISH STEW MADE WITH VENISON

Soak 2 lbs. rib of venison in salt water for an hour. Cook meat slowly for about two hours in sufficient water to cover it. Put aside till cold and remove all the fat. Add 2 lbs. mixed root vegetables prepared and sliced and boil for half an hour. Then add 2 lbs. raw scrubbed potatoes and simmer till potatoes are cooked.

FOR A NOT-SO-YOUNG CHICKEN

Prepare the bird; rub breast with cut lemon or vinegar. Stuff lightly with chopped raw vegetables. Wrap the bird in greased paper for 1½ hours. Then remove from steamer and put in a baking tin. Spread the breast with a little dripping and cover with margarine papers. Roast in a moderate oven, removing the papers for the last ten minutes—save the water in the steamer for soup.

A tough chicken can be cooked in a casserole. Joint the bird and fry the joints for a minute or two in a little fat to brown them. Put them in a casserole with an onion and any other vegetables, cover with stock, vegetable water or water, and simmer until tender. Serve with savoury stuffing balls.

OFFAL

Few people realise how many kinds of offal there are. Many of them are delicacies, all of them can be made into nourishing and palatable dishes.

Here is a list of offal :—

Ox tongue.	Calves' tongues.	Sheep's sweet-
Ox heart.	Calves' sweet-	breads.
Ox liver.	breads.	Sheep's tongues.
Ox tail.	Calves' head	Sheep's kidneys.
Ox kidney.	(scalded).	Sheep's heads.
Ox skirts.	Calves' hearts.	Pigs' liver.
Ox cheek.	Calves' feet.	Pigs' tongue.
Ox sweetbreads.	Calves' kidneys.	Pigs' hearts
Ox tripe.		Pigs' kidneys.
	Sheep's liver.	
Calves' liver.	Sheep's hearts.	Chitterlings.

PARSLEY TRIPE

1 lb. dressed tripe.	1 bay leaf.
2-3 carrots. [sley.	Dash of vinegar.
3 dessertspoons chopped par-	1 oz. dripping or margarine.
1 oz. flour.	1 teacup of milk.
Salt and pepper.	1 pint water.

Cut the tripe into square pieces and put into a saucepan with the carrots sliced in rings, a pint of water, the bay leaf, salt and pepper to taste. Simmer gently for 1¾ hours.

Melt the margarine in a small saucepan, stir in the flour and cook until it bubbles, stirring all the time. Strain off the stock from the tripe and make the liquid up to a pint with milk. Take the saucepan off the heat and stir in the liquid gradually. Bring to the boil and simmer for at least 3 minutes.

Take out the bay leaf from the stewed tripe. Add the parsley to the sauce, pour over the meat and reheat. Add a little more salt and pepper, if necessary, and a dash of vinegar just before serving.

(Enough for 4 people.)

CURRIED TRIPE

1 lb. dressed and cooked tripe.	1 dessertspoon flour.
2-3 finely minced spring onions.	1 oz. dripping or margarine.
Salt and pepper.	¾ pint vegetable boilings or
1 dessertspoon curry powder.	water.

Cut the tripe into 2-inch squares. Cook gently until tender (about 1½ hours). Melt the dripping in a saucepan, put in the minced onion and cook slowly until it just

begins to turn brown. Add the curry powder and flour
and mix all together. Pour in the vegetable boilings or
water ; stir until smooth, then bring to boil and season
to taste. Put the tripe into this sauce and allow to simmer
gently for about 20 minutes. Serve on a hot dish with a
border of mashed potato.

STEWED TRIPE WITH CELERY

2 lb. dressed tripe.	¾ pint water.
I oz. dripping or margarine.	I oz. flour.
I head of celery cut in small pieces.	I gill milk.
	Salt and pepper.

Cut the tripe in strips or square pieces. Put it into a
saucepan with the dripping. Put the lid on the pan and
cook the contents for ten minutes over a gentle heat,
shaking the pan from time to time. Add the water and
the celery cut into small pieces. Bring to the boil, and
simmer for 1¾ hours. Mix the flour to a thin cream with
a little cold water. Add the hot milk and water from the
saucepan, then pour all back into the saucepan and
bring to the boil. Cook steadily for 5 minutes, stirring
all the time. Season with salt and pepper and serve hot.
(Sufficient for 6-8 persons.)

STUFFED TRIPE

I lb. dressed tripe.	A little milk to bind.
4 oz. breadcrumbs.	½ teaspoon powdered sage.
2 rashers of streaky bacon, if possible.	3-4 chopped spring onions.
	Pepper and salt.

Wash the tripe well and put it in warm water and bring
to the boil. Grease an oven dish and cover the bottom
with one finely diced rasher of bacon. On this spread a
layer of stuffing made from the breadcrumbs mixed with
the sage, onion, and the seasoning moistened with milk.
Take the tripe from the water and cut into convenient
pieces, and fill dish with alternate layers of tripe and
stuffing. Garnish the lot with the second rasher of bacon,
finely diced, and cook in a moderate oven for an hour.
Serve with some good gravy, for which the water in which
the tripe was boiled may be used as a base.
(Sufficient for 4 people.)

BAKED SAVOURY LIVER

I lb. liver.	¾ oz. dripping.
½ teaspoon vegetable extract.	4 oz. breadcrumbs.
I breakfastcup water.	2 dessertspoons parsley.
Mixed herbs.	Salt and pepper.

Place the sliced liver in a greased baking tin and round it pour a breakfastcup of water in which some vegetable extract has been dissolved. Mix breadcrumbs, parsley, herbs, and salt and pepper, and fork in the dripping. Spread each slice of liver with the mixture. Cover tightly with a margarine paper and bake in a moderate oven for half an hour. Remove the paper and brown the crumbs. Add a little more liquid if necessary.

LIVER DUMPLING

Served with a border of mashed potatoes this is very good. Take :

8 oz. liver.	1 tablespoon flour.
2 tablespoons toasted oatmeal.	6 spring onions (finely chopped).
2 tablespoons breadcrumbs.	Salt and pepper.

Stock to mix.

Chop the liver, mix it with oatmeal, flour, chopped onions and breadcrumbs, season with salt and pepper. Add chopped vegetable to make a mixture of the consistency of forcemeat, not too thick, as breadcrumbs and oatmeal will swell. Put in a bowl, cover with greased paper and steam for 2 to 3 hours.

(Enough for 4 people.)

SAVOURY LIVER PUDDING

8 oz. potato suet crust (see p. 59, POTATOES).

Filling.—4 oz. finely chopped liver ; 1 rasher streaky bacon, finely diced, or 1 teaspoonful gravy powder ; pinch of herbs ; finely chopped spring onion, if possible, or 1 sliced tomato.

Make up the potato suet crust in the usual way and roll out into a neat oval. Spread with the meat mixture, trim the edges, roll up and tie with a flour cloth or with margarine paper and steam 2½ hours.

(This serves 3-4 people.)

COW HEEL WITH PARSLEY SAUCE

1 cow heel.	A small bunch of herbs.
Cold water.	1 oz. dripping or margarine.
Handful chopped celery leaves or bunch spring onions.	1 oz. flour.
	1 tablespoon chopped parsley.

Salt and pepper.

Wash and scrape the heel and cut it into four, removing fat from between the hoof pieces. Put in a saucepan with cold water to cover, bring to the boil, and pour the water away, rinsing the saucepan and the heel until rid of all scum. Put the heel on again with cold water to cover it and bring to the boil. Skim if necessary, add the onions or celery leaves and the bunch of herbs, put the lid on the pan and simmer slowly until tender (3 to 4 hours). If the water boils away, more must be added.

When ready, drain, keeping the liquid. Now prepare the sauce. Melt the butter in the saucepan, add the flour, and mix well in, cooking for a minute or two. Pour in half a pint of liquid from the cow heel, and stir until boiling. Season to taste, add the parsley, and a little milk if the sauce is too thick. Remove the flesh from the bones and cut in small pieces; warm these in the sauce and then serve. (Serves 4 people.)

STEWED OX CHEEK

I ox. cheek.	A bunch of herbs.
I parsnip.	I oz. margarine.
2 or 3 carrots.	I oz. flour.
I small turnip.	Salt and pepper.

Wash the cheek well in warm water, then put in a saucepan, cover with cold water, bring to the boil and skim thoroughly. Add the vegetables, sliced, and the herbs and seasoning. Stew very slowly, keeping just enough liquid in the pan to cover, for 3 to 4 hours, or until the bones come away from the cheek easily.

Melt the margarine in a pan, mix in the flour smoothly, cook for two or three minutes, then add slowly 1 pint of the liquid from the pan and boil up-stirring all the time. Season if necessary.

Remove the bones from the meat, pour on the sauce and simmer together for 10 minutes before serving.

HOT POTATO AND KIDNEY PIES

8 oz. potato pastry (see p. 59).	About I lb. potatoes.
8 oz. ox kidney.	Pinch herbs.
Salt and pepper.	

Remove fat and skin from kidney—cut it into small pieces. Dice the potatoes and mix together with herbs and seasoning. Add a good tablespoon water. Roll out the crust thinly, cut into sufficient rounds to use two for each pie. Grease good-sized deep patty pans, line with pastry, then fill with kidney mixture. Damp edges well, and cover with another round of pastry, pressing edges well together so the juice will not escape. Brush over with milk. Prick a hole in centre of each, and bake in moderately hot oven for about 30-35 minutes, or longer if necessary. Test filling with skewer.

(Serves 4-6 people.)

PIG'S OR SHEEP'S TROTTER

These are often sold ready cooked. If you buy them raw, wash them well, then boil for 1 hour and skin. Place them in clean cold salted water, flavoured with a bay leaf or bunch of herbs, or an onion if you have it, and simmer for 4 hours. You can eat them hot or cold.

BRAWN

½ pig's head or sheep's head. | ½ lb. shin of beef.
Bouquet of herbs or fresh tarra- | 3 cloves.
    goa or 1 onion. | 2-3 peppercorns.

Get the butcher to clean the head for you. Soak it overnight. Steam the beef and the head in a saucepan very slowly with the herbs, peppercorns and cloves, and go on boiling till the meat comes off the bones. Boil with the lid off to reduce the water. Remove the bones. Mash up the meat well, especially the fat. Add enough stock to moisten. Press it into moulds which have been rinsed with cold water. If you have one, put a hard-boiled egg in each mould, pressing it well down. Leave to set. Leave the liquid in the pan to get quite cold. Skim off the fat and use it for cooking. The liquid is good for soup.

SHEEP'S HEAD ROLL

1 sheep's head. | 1 tablespoon vinegar.
4 oz. fine oatmeal. | 1 faggot of sweet herbs.
4 oz. browned breadcrumbs. | 2 cloves, tiny blade of mace.
1 lb. carrots. | 5 peppercorns, a bruised chili
1 lb. swede and turnip. | and a piece of nutmeg.
1 onion or a leek or a few spring | 1 good tablespoon coarse salt.
    onions. | A few drops of catsup.

Sheep's head is still off the ration. Here is a good recipe :

Well cleanse the sheep's head in salted water and then rinse. Tie the head up to keep in the brains. Bring quickly to the boil in plain water and throw this water away. Put the head on again in a deep pan of water. Add vinegar, salt, the spice and herbs tied in a muslin bag, and all the vegetables, cut in convenient pieces. Cook gently till the meat is ready to leave the bone.

Lift out the head and, when cool enough to handle, remove every scrap of meat. Dip the tongue in cold water, skin it, slice the tongue in neat wafers. Put the other meat through the mincer together with the vegetables, the oatmeal and crumbs. This makes perfect blending easy.

Now taste for flavour and add a few drops of catsup or Worcestershire sauce if needed. While all this is being done the liquor should be boiling fast to reduce. Strain a little of it off to bind your meat and vegetable mixture. Form the mixture into a roll with the sliced tongue down the centre. Divide into two and pack into two greased jam-jars. Cover with grease-proof and steam, or cook in the wet oven, for about 1 hour. Turn out when cold and roll in golden crumbs mixed with a little finely chopped mint or parsley. Serve hot with piquant sauce and plenty of mixed vegetables, or cold with salad.

BAKED STUFFED SHEEP'S HEART

4 sheep's hearts.   2 oz. dripping.

1 teacup breadcrumbs.	1 small onion minced or finely
1 teaspoon mixed herbs.	chopped.
1 tablespoon chopped suet or	Salt, pepper, milk to bind.
dripping (if possible.)	Finely chopped parsley.

Mix ingredients of stuffing together in a basin. Cleanse hearts thoroughly, cutting away pipes and flaps. Soak in lukewarm salted water for ½ hour. Dry well.

Fill the cavities with stuffing, and sew up ; or tie over a strong piece of greased paper to keep the stuffing in place. Place in a saucepan with about 2 inches of water and simmer slowly 1 hour.

Melt the dripping in the baking tin, put in the hearts and baste them well, baking them in a moderate oven for ¾ hour.

To serve: snip the threads, slice neatly, and serve with good thickened gravy.

(These quantities are sufficient for 5-6 people.)

SHEEP'S HEAD BROTH

1 sheep's head. 2 carrots.	1 onion (if possible).
2 tablespoons pearl barley.	Pepper and salt.
3 quarts cold water.	1 tablespoon chopped parsley.
1 turnip.	2 sticks of celery.

Ask your butcher to dress and clean the head for you and be sure that he sends you the brains and the tongue.

Take out the brains and save for sauce or a separate savoury. Wash the head and tongue thoroughly, and let them soak in cold water with a handful of salt in it for 1 hour or more. Then put the head and tongue in a large saucepan with cold water to cover them, and a little salt, bring to the boil, pour this water away, and rinse the head and refill the saucepan with clean water.

Put the head back in the saucepan with the barley, a little salt, and 3 quarts of cold water. Bring to the boil and skim well. Add the turnip, carrot, onion, and celery cut into neat pieces. Simmer slowly for $3\frac{1}{2}$ hours. Add the parsley at the last, with pepper, and more salt if necessary. (Enough for 5-6 people.)

The head may be lifted out and served as a separate dish with parsley or brain sauce poured over it. Or, as much as seems desirable of the meat may be cut in small pieces and served in the soup. The tongue should always be skinned before being used.

BRAINS ON TOAST

Wash the brains well in salted water, tie in muslin, and boil in salted water for about 10 minutes. Cut into neat pieces, put on toast, and cover with parsley sauce or mustard sauce, to which a dash of vinegar has been added. (Enough for 4.)

WAYS WITH CORNED BEEF

When you are offered corned beef instead of your usual cut of meat, do you know how to make it into a substantial dish? The great point is to keep it moist and use its fat to the best advantage. Here is a suggestion from America :

POTATO AND CORNED BEEF PANCAKE

Mix together 1 breakfastcup of chopped corned beef with the same quantity of diced raw potato, and season with pepper and salt. Pour into a frying pan $\frac{3}{4}$ of a teacup milk or stock and a teaspoon of dripping or cooking fat. When warmed, put in the meat and potatoes, spreading them evenly. Dot another teaspoon of fat over the top. Place a plate over the pan and allow the pancake to cook *quite slowly* for about 45 minutes. A thick delicious crust will form on the bottom. Fold the pancake across and serve it up on a hot dish with cooked green vegetables.

CORNED BEEF AND OATMEAL PUDDING

1 lb. chopped corned beef.	1 oz. dripping.
4 oz. fine oatmeal.	2 tablespoons grated raw carrot.
2 oz. wheatmeal breadcrumbs.	$\frac{1}{2}$ pint stock or vegetable water.
1 teaspoon powdered sage.	Pepper and salt.

Toast oatmeal lightly in the dripping, add the other ingredients, mix all together with the stock. Turn into a greased basin, and boil or steam for 1½ hours. Serve with green vegetables.

PANNED CORNED BEEF AND BEETROOT

1 cup chopped corned beef.	Diced spring onions.
1½ cups cooked and diced potato.	Seasoning—Pepper and salt.
1 cup diced cooked beetroot.	Grated apple or horseradish sauce.

Vegetable stock to moisten.

Mix the diced potato and corned beef together, season well with pepper and salt and 3 teaspoons of finely diced spring onion. Moisten to a creamy consistency with a little stock or vegetable boilings and turn into a hot greased frying pan thick enough to hold the heat well.

Spread evenly like a pancake and brown slowly for about 25 to 30 minutes over a steady low heat.

Serve with an outer ring of diced pan-fried beetroot (cooked alongside in a saucepan) topped with grated apple or horseradish sauce and a sprig of chopped parsley.

FATS

Here are some ways in which we can eke out fats to make them serve us best.

Trim away the outer rim of fat from chops or cuts of meat. Render it down and clean it for use in frying, in making cakes or pastry. Fat is often wasted when it could become a valuable addition to supplies from the kitchen.

After boiling fatty meats and suet puddings, allow the liquid to stand overnight to get cold. The skimmings can be used for shallow frying. Allow them to heat through slowly first, until the water has evaporated.

Another way of using up trimmings of fat is to chop them finely and frizzle them in the frying pan. The fat will cook small portions of meat or fry fish-cakes. Do not forget to serve the crisp kernels too ; they are delicious.

Bacon rind, chopped finely, is good when the fat has been extracted from it. Try this in soups or as an addition to potato salad.

Remember to use the wrapping-papers from margarine and other fats for greasing dishes and covering food in the oven.

Fats left in the frying pan can be strained free of crumbs and used again.

OATMEAL

SCOTLAND gives us oatmeal, the most valuable of all our cereals, more nourishing even than wheatmeal flour. Oatmeal is one of the simple foods on which our forefathers lived and throve. The cakes that King Alfred burned were, in all probability, oaten cakes, and for many a century oatmeal played an important part in the countryman's diet. During the last hundred years other cereals have tended to oust it from the Englishman's table, but to-day it is coming into its own again.

Why is oatmeal valuable? Because it not only builds our bodies and gives us energy but also helps to protect us from illness. Oatmeal contains even more of that elusive vitamin B1 than wholemeal bread and far away more than white flour. That is one reason why it is a " protective " food. Another is that it gives us the elements that make bone and blood.

What can we make with oatmeal? Porridge and oatcakes certainly, but there are many other ways of using it. It is excellent when added to many meat and vegetable dishes, and can be used to thicken soups and stews. It makes a delicious stuffing for meat and poultry. Fish, especially herrings, are very good cooked in oatmeal. It can replace some of the white flour in scones, cakes, biscuits and puddings. Last, but not least, oatmeal water is a refreshing drink.

Choose medium oatmeal or rolled oats for porridge, biscuits and puddings. Fine oatmeal is excellent for coating fish and rissoles, while the coarse is usually preferred for stuffings. When making scones and bread you will need some flour to supply the necessary gluten.

Don't forget that oatmeal contains fat, so that it will not keep indefinitely. It will keep for a month or two if stored in a tightly lidded container, but take care to use it all up before you put in a new supply.

For thickening soups and stews—allow 1½ to 2 oz. oatmeal for every two pints to be thickened. This should be added to the soup or stew about 30 minutes before serving. Fine, medium or coarse oatmeal may be used.

TO MAKE PORRIDGE

2 oz. medium oatmeal. | 1 pint water.
Pinch salt.

Bring the water to the boil, add the salt, and sprinkle in the oatmeal slowly, stirring all the time. Take care that the water does not go off the boil. Simmer and stir for five minutes, then simmer for 45 minutes, stirring occasionally.

If you have a double saucepan cook your porridge in it, as it can be left to cook by itself with only an occasional stirring.

A hay-box is also excellent for porridge. After the first five minutes' boiling, put your saucepan in the hay-box and leave for at least $1\frac{1}{2}$ hours, or all night if you prefer. Heat up again before serving.

In Scotland oatmeal porridge is sometimes cooked for a few minutes only, and where this type of porridge is liked it certainly saves fuel. Another good method is to mix the oatmeal to a paste with the cold water, let it stand overnight and then cook for 15 minutes only.

OATMEAL DUMPLINGS

To accompany soup or stew

4 oz. medium oatmeal.	Herbs, or suitable flavouring,
4 oz. self-raising flour.	minced onion, etc.
1 oz. grated suet or dripping.	Water for mixing to a stiff
Level teaspoon salt.	dough.

Pepper.

Mix the dry ingredients, then add suet or fat, and the seasonings and flavourings. Mix to a stiff consistency with cold water, divide into equal portions, and with floured hands form into balls. Drop into soup or stew and cook under closely fitting lid for half an hour before the dish is required.

MEALIE GRACHIE

$\frac{1}{2}$ lb. medium oatmeal.	Pinch mixed herbs or celery
Dripping from bacon or	salt.
sausages.	About $\frac{1}{2}$ teacup of water.

Salt, pepper.

Toast the oatmeal by tossing it to and fro in a clean saucepan over low heat. Empty out the oatmeal into a basin. Put in the pan some fat which has been saved from frying bacon or sausages. Work in the toasted oatmeal until it has completely absorbed the fat.

Season well with salt and pepper, then add a flavouring of mixed herbs or celery salt. Boil the water and pour it over the meal so that it swells. Mix it thoroughly by turning over quickly before the water evaporates. When thoroughly hot, turn into a heated dish and serve.

MEALIE PUDDING (" Donkey ")

1 breakfastcup medium Scotch oatmeal (½ pint).	1 large onion or 2 leeks.
2 oz. chopped suet.	Salt. Cold water.

Chop the onion or leeks finely and blend well with the oatmeal, suet, pepper and salt. Mix with a pint of cold water to a soft dough.

Put into a greased basin, leaving plenty of room for it to swell, and steam for three hours. Turn out and serve hot or cold.

LIVER AND ROLLED OATS HOT-POT

8 oz. thinly sliced and chopped raw liver (or raw minced meat).	½ pint household stock or vegetable extract dissolved in ½ pint water.
2 oz. raw rolled oats.	Sliced raw potato to cover the dish.
A little minced onion, if available (or chopped spring onion, or onion essence).	Salt, pepper. Mixed herbs.

Grease a pie-dish, then layer the sliced liver with sprinkled rolled oats and good seasoning, pinch mixed herbs and the onion, if used.

Fill up with the stock, and cover the top with sliced raw potato in overlapping arrangement. Lay a margarine paper over the top and place in a moderate oven to bake slowly for 1½ hours.

SAVOURY OATMEAL BAKE

4 oz. medium oatmeal.	About 1 teacup vegetable boilings in which a little vegetable extract has been dissolved.
4 oz. wheatmeal breadcrumbs.	
2½ oz. suet.	
1 rounded teaspoon salt.	
1 tomato (in season) or pinch herbs.	Pepper.
2 teaspoons chopped parsley.	Minced spring onion, if possible, finely diced.

Soak the bread, squeeze dry and beat until light with a fork. Add the other dry ingredients and mix well. Season and bind with the stock.

Turn into a greased tin and bake in a moderately hot oven for 40 minutes. Cut into sections and serve hot or cold. *In finger lengths, this savoury bake is a good accompaniment to a bowl of soup for the shelter meal, or a portable lunch, when soup is carried in a vacuum flask.*

OATMEAL FISH ROLLS

4 oz. cooked fish.	A little minced onion, chopped
1 teacup of stiff cooked porridge.	spring onion or onion
1 teacup of mashed potatoes.	flavouring.
Pepper and salt.	Chopped parsley.

Fine oatmeal for coating.

Flake the fish finely, removing all skin and bone, and mix it in smoothly with the porridge. Add seasonings, chopped parsley and the onion. Then work in the mashed potatoes until evenly mixed and of firm texture.

Divide into even portions, form into rolls, and coat in the fine oatmeal. Fry in hot fat till golden brown and serve with sauté potatoes or oatcake for breakfast, or with a good sauce and vegetables for the main dish of the day.

BAKED FISH AND OATMEAL BALLS

1 lb. cod or ling.	1 oz. dripping.
1 cup milk.	1 teacup oatmeal ($\frac{1}{4}$ lb.)
A little chopped parsley.	Minced onion.
$\frac{1}{4}$ teaspoon salt.	Pepper.

Wash the fish, and place it in the dish with the milk and seasonings. Mix other ingredients and form into a stiff dough, and then divide and form into balls. Bake them round the fish for $\frac{1}{2}$-$\frac{3}{4}$ hour.

BROSE

1 turnip.	Oatmeal (toasted).
1 or 2 carrots.	Seasoning.
$\frac{1}{4}$ cabbage.	Meaty bone (optional).

Prepare and slice a turnip, a few carrots and the cabbage, and include any other vegetables you may happen to have. Place them in a pan with a meaty bone, if liked, cover with cold water, add a pinch of salt and simmer until they are tender.

Place a handful of toasted oatmeal in each soup bowl, add a pinch of pepper and salt, and a small piece of margarine. Now add a ladleful of stock from the pan while still boiling and stir. (Original Scotch brose forms "knots.") When evenly mixed, serve hot. The vegetables themselves can be served for the next course.

OATMEAL BREAD

2 cups fine oatmeal.	2 breakfastcups sour milk (or
2$\frac{1}{2}$ breakfastcups flour.	buttermilk if obtainable).
$\frac{1}{2}$ teaspoon salt.	1 teaspoon bicarbonate of soda.

Steep the oatmeal in the sour milk or buttermilk overnight. Sift the flour, salt and bicarbonate of soda together and stir into the oatmeal until you have a stiff dough. If necessary, add a little more sour milk.

Turn on to a floured board and knead lightly until smooth. Roll out about 2 inches thick, cut into four and bake in a moderate oven for 25 minutes.

OATCAKES (Traditional Recipe)

Mix 1 lb. of oatmeal with some lukewarm water to form a stiff dough. Add a pinch of salt.

Roll out thinly, bake on a girdle, or on iron plates placed over a slow fire, for three or four minutes, then place before the fire to harden.

Keep the oatcakes in a dry place and they will be good for months.

OATCAKES (Using Fat)

8 oz. oatmeal.	1½ oz. self-raising flour.
1 tablespoon dripping.	½ teaspoon salt.

Some boiling water.

Mix the oatmeal, flour and salt together. Add the melted dripping and enough boiling water to bind. Knead the dough until free from cracks. Roll out as thinly as possible on a board sprinkled with oatmeal.

Cut into triangles and bake on a greased tin in a fairly hot oven.

OATMEAL SCONES, OR FARLS

1 lb. oatmeal.	1 small teaspoon salt.
2-3 oz. margarine, dripping, or fat.	About ¼ pint of new milk or milk and water.
¼ lb. self-raising flour.	

Place the oatmeal, flour, salt, etc., into a bowl. Rub in the margarine with the tips of the fingers and mix to a very stiff dough with the milk. Knead lightly on a floured board till smooth. Roll out about half an inch thick, then cut into triangle shapes. They can be baked either on a greased girdle or in the oven.

PORRIDGE SCONES

½ lb. cold porridge.	¼ lb. flour.
¼ lb. oatmeal.	1 teaspoon bicarbonate of soda.
½ teaspoon salt.	2 teaspoons cream of tartar.

Mix all the dry ingredients and work in the cold porridge. Roll out to a depth of about ½ inch, cut into rounds and cook on a hot girdle, or roll rather thicker, cut as before, and bake in a hot oven.

OATMEAL DRINK (Cold)

3 pints water. | 2 oz. oatmeal. | ½ oz. sugar.

Boil the ingredients together. Do not strain. Shake well before drinking.

This can be diluted if necessary, but the water added should be boiled first.

SOUP

A NOURISHING soup is a meal in itself. And a very comforting meal. Well prepared, it can be warmed up in a few minutes for any emergency.

You can take it in a vacuum flask to the Air Raid Shelter. You can leave it ready to be heated when you return after the All Clear.

Soup saves you time—and money—now.

You will find the water in which potatoes and other vegetables have been cooked an excellent foundation.

It is a great mistake to think that a bone stock is necessary for soup. Bones, with the exception of marrow bones, give flavour but no nourishment. Try making soups from vegetables only, and remember that if you grate the root vegetables and chop the green ones, the soup will cook in 20 minutes.

A vegetable soup thickened with oatmeal or with oatmeal dumplings added (see p. 97) is a meal in itself.

A little milk when it can be spared adds to the value of a soup.

Hard cheese rinds, which do not yield enough gratings for other purposes, will produce a spoonful to sprinkle over a hot soup. This makes it more interesting and adds to the food value.

SIMPLE BREAD SOUP (Quick)

Dry in the oven a few slices of stale bread till well coloured and crush them finely.

Boil ½ pint of milk in 1 pint water and season with pepper and salt. Add 2 teacups of breadcrumbs to the soup, stir well, and cook over a good heat till swollen. Add 2 tablespoons of finely chopped parsley.

QUICK SOUP

1 pint vegetable boilings or water.	½ oz. dripping.
A tablespoon of cooked porridge and 1 teacup milk, if liked.	About ¼ lb. mixed vegetables—carrot, turnip, stick of celery, potato, etc., with 1 or 2 spring onions.

Prepare the vegetables, then grate the root vegetables and toss them for a few minutes in the hot dripping over low heat, with the lid on the pan. Add the diced spring onions and heat for another minute—5 minutes in all.

Add a pinch of salt, pour on the hot liquid, replace the lid and simmer for about 15 minutes, until the vegetables are tender. Serve at once. Or thicken by mixing the made porridge with the cold milk and adding to the boiling soup, boil up and serve.

RAW BEETROOT SOUP

1 lb. grated raw beetroot.	1 oz. flour to thicken.
1 quart vegetable boilings or water.	Apple peelings or a little vinegar to taste.

Salt and pepper.

Simmer the grated beetroot in the salted vegetable stock with a very little vinegar or some apple peelings.

At the end of 20 to 25 minutes the beetroot will be tender. Strain and thicken it by mixing the flour to a smooth cream with a little cold water and adding some of the boiling stock to it, stirring as it thickens. Return all to the saucepan and simmer, stirring for 7 to 10 minutes. Season and serve very hot.

BEETROOT AND CABBAGE SOUP (Quick)

1 small cup of cooked or grated raw cabbage.	1½ pints vegetable stock or water.
1 small cooked beetroot.	Salt and pepper.
Parsley, thyme, bay leaf, etc.	1 teaspoon vegetable extract (optional).

Chop the cabbage and dice the beetroot. Boil up the vegetable stock with the herbs, add the vegetables and simmer 15 minutes. Remove the herbs, stir in the vegetable extract, check the seasoning and serve. Sharpened with a trace of lemon juice or vinegar, the flavour is extra good.

STRAIGHT-FROM-THE-GARDEN SOUP (Quick)

4 oz. shelled green peas.	1 quart of vegetable boilings or water.
3 oz. French beans.	
2 young turnips (about 2½ oz.).	2 oz. lettuce or spring greens.
Sprig of mint.	3 tender carrots (about 2½ oz.).
1 onion.	3 oz. spinach.
1½ oz. rice.	Seasoning.

Wash and prepare the vegetables, dicing the root vegetables and beans, and shredding the greens finely.

Simmer the stock, add the washed rice, with vegetables, and boil for 20 minutes, or until all the vegetables are tender. Season well, remove the mint, and serve very hot.

GOLDEN SOUP

I lb. potato.	Golden outer skins from 2 medium-sized onions.
1¾ pints water or vegetable boilings.	¾ oz. flour.
I gill milk.	Chopped parsley.

Bay leaf.

Cook the well-scrubbed and sliced potatoes in the boiling salted water with the onion skins and bay leaf. When pulped, stir the flour to a smooth cream with the cold milk. Pour on a little boiling soup and return it to the pan. Stir while it boils, remove the bay leaf. Sprinkle with a dessertspoon of chopped parsley. Season and serve hot.

BARLEY BROTH

½ lb. of lean scrag or middle neck of mutton.	6 spring onions—or, if you have it, I small leek.
I quart water.	2 small turnips or piece of swede.
I oz. pearl barley.	A muslin bag of mixed herbs.
3 or 4 good-sized carrots.	

Chopped parsley.

Trim the fat and the meat, then place in a saucepan with the cold water, muslin of herbs, pearl barley and salt, and the diced spring onions. Bring slowly to the boil, then add the diced carrot and turnip. Simmer for about 1¼ hours, then take out the meat and remove the flesh from the bones, cutting the meat finely before returning it to the broth. Heat again, adding more seasoning if necessary, and serve with a sprinkling of finely chopped parsley.

This broth is also good served with little oatmeal dumplings in place of the barley. Drop into the soup about ¼ hour before it is to be served. (See p. 97, OAT-MEAL.)

POLISH BARLEY SOUP

I quart vegetable boilings.	turnips, celery, parsnip, spring onion or leek. Kale, cauliflower. Mushrooms or stalks if available.
I oz. pearl barley.	
I lb. mixed vegetables—potatoes, carrots, swedes or	

Chopped parsley.

Simmer the diced vegetables in the boiling salted liquor with the barley until tender. In Poland sour cream would be added, but we can use a little milk as a finish if we have it. Sprinkle with parsley before serving.

A bowl of this soup served with toast, oven-dried rusks or crisp rolls would make a meal.

CARROT AND OATMEAL SOUP

1 lb carrots.	½ oz. fine oatmeal.
Outside sticks of a head of celery.	A few bacon rinds or 1 oz. fat.
	Pepper and salt.

Pinch of nutmeg—if liked.

Scrape the carrots and cut into rings. Wash the celery and cut into inch lengths. Frizzle the bacon rinds, or melt the fat in the saucepan, and put in the carrots and celery and cook gently for about 5 minutes, shaking occasionally.

Add 1½ pints of water and simmer for one hour. Mash the vegetables to a pulp with the blunt end of a rolling pin. Remove the bacon rinds and any stringy pieces of celery.

Blend the oatmeal with a little water and add to the soup. Bring to the boil and simmer for 10 to 15 minutes, then season and serve with bread rusks—made by baking the ends of the loaf, or any left-over bread, in the oven till quite crisp.

SWEDE SOUP

1½ lb. swedes.	2 pints water.
1 heaped tablespoon flour or fine oatmeal.	½ pint milk.
Small piece of dripping.	Chopped spring onion and bacon rinds if possible.

Wash and pare the swedes, then cut them into small pieces. Melt the fat in a pan, add the bacon and chopped onion, then the swedes, and cook gently for 6 to 7 minutes. Add the water and 2 teaspoons salt, and simmer until the vegetables are quite soft.

Strain the stock into a bowl, and mash the swedes with a fork against the sides of the pan. Blend the flour with a little of the milk, then return stock, milk, and paste to the pan, bring to the boil, stirring all the while. Cook 15 minutes, season with pepper and a grating of nutmeg. Serve very hot.

GREEN PEA SOUP

1 lb. peas in pod.	1 small onion, or spring onions.
A few sprigs of mint.	1 oz. cooking fat or dripping.
1 oz. flour or fine oatmeal.	1 quart stock or water.

Salt and pepper.

Shell the peas and wash the pods well, rejecting any that are not clear skinned or fresh. Melt the fat, and fry the skinned and minced onion, to draw the flavour. Add the

flour or oatmeal and stir to blend, then allow to bubble
and spread a little. Pour on the water, stirring until
smooth, then add the pea pods, mint sprigs and a little
salt. Simmer until the pods are tender, about 50 minutes
to an hour.

Pass through a wire sieve and return the soup to the
saucepan, bring it to the boil again. Add the green peas
and simmer until tender. Season with pepper, salt if
necessary, and a pinch of sugar. Serve very hot.

CELERY SOUP

1 large head of celery.
1½ pints white stock.
1 oz. dripping.
½ pint milk.

1 onion, if possible, or diced
   spring onion.
1 tablespoon fine oatmeal.
Salt, pepper.

Clean and cut up the celery. Slice the peeled onion,
or cut the spring onions into fine rings. Sauté the diced
vegetables in a little heated fat, then pour on the water,
cover and cook steadily until tender. A little salt draws
out the flavours in the simmering.

Blend the oatmeal in the milk smoothly, pour on a little
of the soup, then return all to the saucepan to thicken.
Cook, stirring occasionally, for 15 minutes, then season
and serve.

MIXED VEGETABLE SOUP

2 carrots.
1 medium turnip.
2 small onions, if available, or
   diced spring onion.
1½ pints vegetable stock.

Either ¼ head of celery or 2
   leeks (replacing onion), or
   ¼ swede or 2 potatoes.
1 oz. dripping.
1 oz. fine oatmeal or flour.

½ pint milk.

Prepare the vegetables, then cut up fairly small and
cook until tender. (If time allows, sauté them first in
the heated dripping, to draw the flavours.)

Mix the oatmeal or flour to a smooth paste with the
milk, pour on to it some of the hot stock, then return all
to the saucepan to stir until the flour thickens. Boil for
15 minutes. Season well, and serve very hot.

CAULIFLOWER SOUP

1 medium-sized cauliflower.
1 oz. ground rice or cornflour.

1 pint cold milk.
1¼ pints cauliflower liquor.

Seasoning.

Cook the cauliflower in 1¼ pints boiling salted water
until tender. Take out the cauliflower and chop finely.

Thicken the water with the ground rice or cornflour, mixed with a little cold water to a smooth paste. Allow to simmer, stirring until thickened, then replace the cauliflower to heat through. Add milk, pepper and salt if necessary, and serve very hot.

PEASANT SOUP

2 pints stock.
1 large potato.
1 turnip.
A little minced onion, or diced spring onion.

1 carrot.
A few sticks of macaroni.
2 tomatoes (in season).
Grated cheese—if available.
Seasoning.

A little shredded cabbage.

Wash and prepare the vegetables, cutting potato, carrot and turnip into small cubes. Add these to the stock and bring to the boil, with minced onion. Simmer gently for 10 minutes, then add the macaroni broken into short lengths, the sliced tomatoes, and the shredded cabbage.

Simmer gently until the vegetables are tender, then season to taste.

SPINACH SOUP

1½ lbs. spinach.
1 oz. dripping or margarine.
1 oz. flour.

1 gill milk.
1½ pints vegetable stock or water.

Nutmeg, salt, pepper.

Thoroughly wash the spinach in several waters. Put it in a large pan with the water clinging to the leaves, and allow it to cook slowly until the juice begins to draw.

Add the salt, pepper and nutmeg, and cook steadily until tender (about 10 minutes).

Lift the spinach on to a board and chop it well with a sharp knife.

Make up a sauce with the fat, flour and hot milk. When this is thoroughly smooth, add it to the pan together with the vegetable stock or water and the chopped spinach.

Boil for another 10 minutes and serve piping hot.

PEA POD SOUP

Wash the pods thoroughly, choosing good clear skins, and place them in a deep pan. Add washed sliced vegetables to requirements—carrots, turnips, onions, etc.— and cover all with cold water. Replace the lid and cook slowly until tender.

Puree the vegetables through a sieve, then return to the pot. Blend a little cornflour (1 oz. to each quart) with cold milk, and add some of the hot soup to it. Return all to the saucepan, and stir until boiling and the soup is creamy. Season with pepper and salt, and serve very hot.

LEEK POTTAGE (Brotchan Roy)

1 oz. medium oatmeal.	1 tablespoon chopped parsley.
1 pint chopped leeks.	1½ pints liquid (milk and water,
1 oz. dripping.	stock or vegetable boilings).
Pinch of powdered mace.	Pepper and salt.

If fat is available, place a piece of dripping in the saucepan. Put in the oatmeal, and fry until it is nearly coloured and has a nutty flavour. Alternatively, toast the oatmeal in the oven.

Next add the liquid, and when it reaches the boil, add the cleaned leeks, prepared as for broth, with the green cut up finely. Replace the lid and simmer until the leeks are cooked, about 45 minutes. Add finely chopped parsley 5 minutes before serving.

Other green-topped vegetables can be substituted for the leeks—par-cooked nettle tops, purple sprouting broccoli or scallions are also good.

CABBAGE AND CELERY SOUP

1 small cabbage.	1½ dessertspoons flour.
Half a head of celery.	Pepper and salt.
Bunch of herbs.	1 oz. dripping.
1¾ pints water.	Good pinch allspice or grate of
¼ pint milk.	nutmeg.

Wash and prepare the cabbage and celery, then shred them finely. Melt the dripping in the saucepan and add the vegetables. Sauté slowly, and fry without colouring for a few minutes.

Add the water, or vegetable boilings, with pepper, salt, and flavourings with herb bag, and simmer till the vegetables are tender—about 40 minutes.

When very tender, pass the vegetables through a coarse sieve, or break up in a colander with a wooden spoon, and return to the saucepan. Thicken by creaming the flour with a little of the cold milk, and adding a little hot soup before bringing all to the boil again. Stir till smoothly thickened, taste for seasoning, add the remaining measure of milk, reheat and serve. A few diced and crisped bacon rinds are a delicious addition, if they can be spared.

CREOLE SOUP

1 small cabbage.	Pepper.
1 medium-sized potato.	Small knob of margarine.
1½ gills water.	Grating of nutmeg.
	1 teacup milk.

Prepare and shred the cabbage finely, then add to the water which has been slightly salted. Cook about half an hour, then add the potato cut into thin slices, and boil a further half-hour, making one hour in all.

Mash the potato into the pureed cabbage with a wooden spoon against the side of the saucepan. Season well with pepper, grate of nutmeg, and add a small knob of margarine. Add the milk and a little more water to bring to the required consistency. Bring to the boil and serve.

KOLDUNY (Dumplings)

½ lb. self-raising flour.	1 oz. dripping or margarine.
	1 oz. mashed potato.

Rub the fat into the flour, then add the mashed potato. Mix to a pliable stiff dough and roll out thinly. Cut into 4-inch rounds with a plain cutter and fill the centre of each with a spoonful of simple savoury mixture—like a turnover. Moisten the edges and close very tightly. Poach the kolduny in a closed saucepan of boiling salted water and vegetable stock until they rise to the top.

Make suitable fillings of wheatmeal breadcrumbs soaked in milk or broth and beaten up with cooked brains, and good seasoning of herbs, pepper and salt. Grated carrot or choppings of bacon trimmings make other good fillings.

For added flavour use vegetable extract, or chopped parsley or chives and other fresh herbs. Bind the mixture chosen with a very little beaten egg or milk.

FRUIT SOUPS.

For summer-time, a cold fruit soup is refreshing. It can be made from any ripe fruit, preferably of the berried variety.

Allow 1 lb. of fruit to every quart of soup required, and simmer until the fruit is soft. Then pass it through a sieve and either thicken with a little flour or cornflour, or simmer an ounce of grain—such as sago or semolina—until it turns clear. Finely broken spaghetti or macaroni is also good as a garnish. Stir the soup until the cereal is cooked, then sweeten to taste.

Cinnamon stick or vanilla pod gives extra flavouring. For an apple soup use a little ginger.

Chill the soup and serve as cold as possible.

BREAD AND BAKING

KEEPING BREAD FRESH

In war-time we have to make the most of all the bread we buy. To make it go as far as possible we must not cut a newly baked loaf, but keep it at least 24 hours before slicing it.

Bread keeps best in well-ventilated crocks or special pans with ventilating holes punched at the side. Never leave the lid tightly in position, but slightly aslant to let air circulate properly. A baker's tip is to cover the loaf with a clean linen cloth or tea towel, and lay over this a second dampened cloth. So long as the damp cloth is kept from direct contact with the loaf, the moisture helps to prevent the bread drying out.

Wheatmeal bread keeps better swathed in clean muslin, to prevent it from becoming dry and hardened on the outer crust.

USING STALE BREAD

When using up stale slices of bread, there are several things that we can do with crust and crumb. Dry it off in slices or cut into fancy shapes in the oven when cooking is done. They will slowly crisp to a rusk-like texture, and keep for weeks in an airtight tin. The children love them with soup or a little stewed fruit. Any that remain can be crushed down and used for coating or toppings.

Not-so-stale crumb is good for lightening sweets of the charlotte type, while wheatmeal crumb is invaluable for bringing up the food value of stuffings for vegetables, fish or meat. (For Au Gratin recipes, see p. 27 and 33.)

Crusts are soon softened for steamed puddings or stuffings if they are soaked a short time with a little cold water, then squeezed in a pudding-cloth and forked in a basin till light and crumbly.

TOAST FOR TEA

For spreading toast directly it is made, use savoury "butters" or potato toppings (see p. 48, POTATOES). For tea-time, try cinnamon toasts with honey, or a little fruit puree, glazed with honey. Fruit can be sprinkled with toasted coarse oatmeal, and browned quickly under the grill to draw the honey flavours.

USING BREAD IN NURSERY SWEETS

SUMMER PUDDING

Slices of stale bread.
1 lb. of summer fruits—raspberries, redcurrants, etc.

Sugar or other sweetening.
Simple custard to serve over the pudding.

Stew the fruit in a very little water, but do not add the sweetening until it is almost cooked.

Place a round of bread in the bottom of a china basin and prepare fingers of bread to line in the sides in charlotte style. Cut several rounds of bread to fit the basin in graduating stages.

Add alternate layers of hot fruit and bread, then pour in the juice, and cover in with a round of bread to fit exactly. Weight down with a saucer and a heavy scale-weight to keep it in place, then leave overnight, or for several hours, to allow the juices to soak up well.

Run a knife round the walls of the mould and turn out carefully. Coat with custard powder sauce and serve cold.

The secret of success with this pudding is to have the fruit really hot.

POOR KNIGHTS' PUDDING

Thickish slices of stale bread.
Pinch of cinnamon.

½ egg beaten up in a cupful of milk, or milk alone.

Dripping for frying.

Mix the cinnamon with the beaten egg and milk. Cut the bread into squares or strips. Dip in the egg and milk and fry carefully in very hot dripping, turning both sides until golden brown.

Drain, and serve at once, spread with a little hot jam or honey and sandwiched together in pairs. If preferred, sprinkle with a very little sugar.

RHUBARB BREAD PUDDING

½ lb. stale bread.
Jam for spreading.
6 sticks of rhubarb.

1 gill water.
1 dessertspoon custard powder.
½ pint milk and water.

Cut the bread into neat thick slices. Spread each with jam. Cut six sticks of rhubarb into 1-inch pieces and stew these in half a breakfast-cup of water until almost tender. Strain the fruit, retaining the liquid, and lay the pieces in the bottom of a pie-dish.

Cover the fruit with a layer of bread-and-jam slices,

add a layer of fruit, then another layer of bread. Pour the rhubarb liquid, which should still be hot, over the bread and fruit and leave to soak half an hour

Mix a dessertspoon of sweetened custard powder smoothly with a little milk and make it up to half a pint with hot milk and water. Pour this uncooked custard mixture into the pie-dish and bake in a moderate oven for 20 minutes. Serve hot or cold.

HOME-MADE BREAD

Home-made bread stays moist and sweet for several days, and there is no need to use fat in the making. Here is a good standard recipe to follow for white bread :—

WHITE BREAD

3½ lb. flour.	1½ pints tepid water.
1 oz. yeast.	3½ teaspoons salt.
1 teaspoon castor sugar.	

For a Quartern Loaf.

Mix the salt and flour, and place in a warm basin in a hot place to heat slightly.

Cream the yeast and sugar together in a slightly warmed basin. The mixture should become liquid. Add the tepid water, which should be just the heat of your little finger.

Make a well in the centre of the warm flour, pour in the liquid and sprinkle a little flour over it. This accelerates the growth of the yeast.

Cover the basin with a warm cloth and put to rise in a warm place for 20 minutes. Then mix the flour and yeast and knead until the dough is smooth and elastic. Put into a floured bowl and leave it covered in a warm place until it doubles its size.

Knead again. Divide the dough into four 1-lb. loaves. Put them in a warm place until the required size is reached. Bake in a hot oven until the loaf is golden brown and sounds hollow if tapped underneath. Cooking time is about ¾-1 hour for a 1-lb. loaf.

BROWN BREAD

Proportions for two 1-lb. loaves.

14 oz. wheatmeal flour.	½ oz. yeast.
14 oz. white flour.	¾ pint tepid water, or milk and
1½ teaspoons salt.	water.
½ teaspoon castor sugar.	

Prepare and cook in the same way as for white bread, but allow to rise for a longer period and "prove" (second rise after shaping the loaves) for about 15 minutes.

QUICKLY MADE BREAD (without Yeast)

1 lb. flour.	1 teaspoon salt.
2 rounded teaspoons baking powder.	Milk or water to mix.
	A little cooking fat if possible.

Sieve the flour, salt, and baking powder to mix well and lighten the flour. Rub the fat into the flour lightly, until evenly mixed.

Add sufficient liquid to work to a soft dough, then turn out on a floured board, and knead lightly and quickly into two shaped loaves. Place on a floured baking tray, and bake in a hot oven for about 40 minutes. To test, reverse the loaf and tap with the knuckles. If it sounds quite hollow, the dough is cooked ; but a dull sound indicates the centre is not sufficiently dried, and the loaf should be returned to the oven for a few minutes more.

For Potato Bread, see p. 58.
For Oatmeal Bread, see p. 99.

SAUCES

A GOOD sauce makes the simplest food seem more interesting. Plain white sauce makes a good foundation for many varieties. This is how you make it :

WHITE SAUCE (coating consistency)

½ pint milk, or milk and vege-	1 oz. flour.
table stock.	1 oz. margarine or clarified fat.
	Seasoning.

For pouring sauces—take ½ oz. each of fat and flour to each half-pint of liquid.

The whole secret of making a smooth sauce is to blend the flour and fat thoroughly before adding the liquid. Melt the fat, then stir in the flour, heat together and allow them to bubble and spread.

Warm the milk but do not boil. Add the milk very gradually to the mixture—off the heat—and stirring all the time. Simmer well after the sauce has thickened, for at least 5 minutes.

Add the seasonings and flavourings you have chosen.

PARSLEY SAUCE.—Add 1 tablespoon of finely chopped parsley.

CAPER SAUCE.—Add 1 tablespoon of chopped capers or pickled nasturtium seeds.

BRAIN SAUCE.—Add 1 sheep's brains cooked and chopped and a few drops of vinegar to sharpen.

MUSTARD SAUCE.—Add 1 teaspoon of dry mustard with the flour.

CELERY SAUCE.—Cook at least one tablespoon of finely grated celery in about 1 gill salted water, strain and use the stock for the sauce with added milk. Finely chopped celery leaves can be added when the sauce is made.

You can make anchovy sauce by adding anchovy essence to taste ; or by adding a quarter of a pound of mushrooms stewed in a little milk, chopped and put in the sauce, you have a different flavouring.

For making sauces quickly, without fat, mix the flour to a smooth cream with a little cold water, or milk, and add some of the boiling liquid to it, stirring all the time. Return all to the saucepan and continue to stir while it thickens and comes to the boil. Simmer for 15 minutes. Season and serve.

MINT SAUCE

2 tablespoons freshly chopped garden mint.
1 teacup of vinegar.

1 dessertspoon warm water.
A little sugar—about 1 teaspoon.

Dissolve the sugar in the warm water. Add the chopped mint and vinegar to it and allow them to stand for about 1 hour. Stir well just before serving.

PIQUANTE SAUCE

For less flavoured Foods.

½ pint brown sauce or thickened gravy.
6-8 peppercorns.
½ bay leaf.
1½ teaspoons vinegar.

1½ teaspoons finely chopped parsley.
1 teaspoon chopped capers, or home-pickled nasturtium seeds.

1 small gherkin, chopped.

Simmer the sauce or gravy with the peppercorns until nicely flavoured. Then strain off and add the other flavouring ingredients and reheat the sauce.

Add the finely chopped parsley a few minutes before serving.

SWEET SAUCES

Use the white sauce recipe above, but replace the seasonings by 2 teaspoons of sugar or 1 teaspoon of honey.

Sauces made with cornflour or custard powder are good with chocolate-flavoured or fruit puddings. Use 1 tablespoon of cornflour or custard powder to each half-pint of milk, or milk and water, if the sauce is required to coat the pudding. Use half measure of cornflour or custard powder if a pouring sauce is required.

Coffee essence makes a change, and coffee custard sauce transforms a plain pudding.

Syrups from bottled or canned fruit are delicious if they are slightly thickened with cornflour, using 1 teaspoon to each half-pint of syrup. When you are opening bottled fruit, remember to save fruit syrups for the children's steamed puddings.

FRUIT

In recent years we have learned to eat and appreciate fruit at almost every meal. Now we depend mainly on fruits of our own growing.

Even a small garden has room somewhere for a line of gooseberry or currant bushes. Plant them to edge a border or to form a dividing-line. Both yield fruits of high Vitamin C content ; both flourish without needing expert attention.

Fruit breakfasts in summer-time are refreshing, and by eating them we save our fish, egg, sausage or bacon for another meal.

Fruit is more valuable uncooked, but for very tart fruits it is sometimes better to reduce the acidity by gentle cooking before sweetening is added. The addition of dry bread or cake crumbs helps to sweeten fruits in summer puddings. Baked batters or steamed suet crust sweets are excellent filled with diced fruit in season, and when the fruit is cooked in the pudding in this way, it requires much less sweetening afterwards.

For serving with stewed fruit, or even a few berries, milk junket is nourishing and excellent, especially for children. Set it in small cups or basins, and when firm the berries, or stewed fruit, can be arranged round the rim.

When using bottled fruits preserved at home with the Campden solution, remember to turn the contents with all the liquid into an open saucepan. Heat them until all the smell of sulphur has been driven off—about 15 minutes. Both fruit and juice are then ready for use.

A SUGAR-SAVING HINT

When you are using acid fruits for stews or pies, it is worth while remembering that you can reduce the sugar needed by as much as one-third by the use of bicarbonate of soda. With stewed fruit add the bicarbonate after cooking and stir it in slowly to avoid frothing. In preparing a pie the bicarbonate should be added before cooking. Raspberries, red currants, plums and rhubarb need half of a level teaspoonful of bicarbonate per pound of raw fruit, gooseberries and black currants a whole level teaspoonful.

An old-fashioned tip for saving sugar is to stew fruit with a piece of bread in the pan. This reduces the acidity.

DOMESTIC PRESERVING

Every bit of garden produce that we cannot eat fresh should be preserved for winter use. Not a scrap should be wasted. Green vegetables may be dried ; beans salted ; apples, pears and plums dried. All kinds of fruit may be pulped or bottled without sugar and will then keep indefinitely.

Full directions for correct preservation methods are contained in the Ministry of Agriculture and Fisheries' " Growmore " Bulletin No. 3, entitled *Preserves from the Garden*, and published by His Majesty's Stationery Office, Price 4d. net through any bookseller.

PACKED MEALS

SANDWICHES are the obvious choice for packed meals.
Vary the obvious choice with some of these suggestions.
They can be packed into small jars and dishes, easy to
carry in a haversack, handkerchief or case.

Try cottage pie or a savoury pudding cooked in a small
jar. You can put chopped gherkin or a little chopped
piccalilli in the cottage pie to give it more flavour, and
it is good eaten cold. Curried vegetables are also good
eaten cold with any green salad.

Try making a jar of potted meat or a simple meat roll
in which the pieces of meat are separate and not pounded
up. This makes the dish more filling.

The sheep's head roll (for which you will find the
recipe on page 92) makes very good substantial sandwiches if cut into slices. Try a jar of potato salad or of
salad made with chopped vegetables, raw or cooked
left-overs mixed together with salad dressing. Try oatcake with home-made spreads.

VEGETABLE TURNOVERS

½ lb. short crust pastry, using 5 oz. National Wheatmeal flour and 3 oz. white flour. | 2 oz. dripping.
| 1 level teaspoon baking powder.
| 1 level teaspoon salt.
½ teaspoon powdered sage.

For the filling.

1½ pints diced or grated vege- | Gravy powder to sprinkle.
tables (cooked). |

Make the pastry by mixing the flours, baking powder
and salt. Then rub in the fat lightly until evenly mixed.
Sprinkle in the half teaspoon of finely powdered sage
and mix with cold water to a stiff dough.

Knead lightly and roll out the dough to one-eighth inch
thickness, then cut into rounds. Brush half the circle of
each with cold water, place a spoonful of the vegetables
in the centre and sprinkle with gravy powder. Fold over
the pastry and press the edges very well together, fluting
them with finger and knife to keep them closed during
cooking.

Arrange them in a baking tin, brush the tops with a
little milk—if you have a few " drainings " handy—and
bake in a brisk oven for 20-25 minutes, according to size.

If liked, the pastry can be made without fat, as for
LORD WOOLTON PIE (see p. 44).

COLD KIDNEY PASTIES

Small rounds of potato pastry. For each pasty, $\frac{1}{4}$ kidney, 1 spring onion, a tablespoon of vegetables diced small, thick gravy. Damp the edges of the pastry rounds, place on the lower half the vegetables tossed in thick gravy, the onion finely minced and the quarter kidney, previously parboiled. Turn over the pastry and firmly crisp the edges to prevent the contents oozing out. Bake in a brisk oven for 10 minutes, lower the heat and cook for 10 minutes more.

Another savoury pasty filling.—2 leeks, 1 rasher of grilled bacon, 1 gill thick white sauce made with half milk and half leek liquid. Slice the white part of the leeks, putting aside the green for soup. Cut the bacon into very small pieces. Mix leek and bacon in the sauce, fill pasties with tablespoonfuls of the mixture.

POTATO AND SAUSAGE SALAD

Potato and carrot.
A pickled gherkin.
A spring onion.
Some thick salad cream.

Small piece of apple and a cold sausage, or a thick slice of liver or smoked sausage, or vegetable galantine.

Dice the potato, carrot and apple. Shred the meat, mince the onion and gherkin.

Toss all the ingredients in salad cream and pack into a carton.

Wrap crisp wheatmeal toast to eat with it.

CARTON MEALS

Save all the cartons you can.

These can be filled with jellied foods which are easy to carry because they do not spill.

To make a jelly that will be firm, but not too stiff, melt 1 oz. gelatine in 1 pint of liquid, using vegetable water to give flavour, and from $\frac{1}{2}$ pint to 1 pint of one of the following :

Diced vegetables in season, shrimps and cucumber, diced lamb's tongue and green peas, flaked fish with cucumber and peas and tomato, any left-overs of minced meat. Pack lettuce leaves to eat with the jellies.

SAVOURY SPREADS

Potato mashed with a teaspoonful of margarine and flavoured with parsley or onion or a little vegetable extract.

Kippers or chopped smoked sprats cooked, flesh taken off the bones, mashed up, with a little mashed potato.

Lettuce or watercress with slices of apple.

Grated carrot (particularly good for children) ; flavoured with a little mayonnaise or salad dressing (for adults).

Grated carrots and shredded cabbage, with a trace of finely chopped celery, bind together well with sweet pickle for a wheatmeal bread sandwich.

Or, if you like *cooked vegetables* in a sandwich, try *carrot cooked in a good curry sauce.*

Here is a substantial filling with cooked vegetables and oatmeal. Grate 1 lb. carrots and cook in boiling salted water, retaining about ½ gill of the " stock." Blend 4 oz. fine oatmeal with a little milk, then add the carrot water and ½ gill milk. Bring to the boil, stirring, and allow to thicken. Slacken to a creamy consistency with a little extra carrot water if necessary. Add ½ oz. finely chopped parsley and a teaspoon of vegetable extract. Season well with pepper and salt, and serve as a hot toast topping, or cold sandwich spread.

Various salad greens make excellent sandwich spreads if they are well chopped and carefully blended with mayonnaise or salad cream of the more economical kind. Try watercress, chopped tender young spinach, young nasturtium leaves and dandelion shoots (young leaves) with lettuce or curly endive.

SALT HERRING SPREAD.

1 salt herring.	½ an apple.

Slice of onion, or 1 spring onion.

Soak the herring in hot water for 5 minutes, remove skin and bones, chop with the apple and onion. Bind with a few drops of salad oil. Spread between slices of wheatmeal bread or in rolls.

LIVER SPREAD.

¼ lb. liver.	Salt.
1 small bay leaf.	6 peppercorns.
1 spring onion.	1 oz. margarine.

Put liver, onion and bay-leaf in sufficient salted water to cover ; bring to the boil, remove scum and cook for 5 minutes only.

Free the meat from any skin, put it twice through the mincer with the onion, using the finest cutters. Warm the margarine, beat it into the liver, add pepper to taste.

This will keep if put into pots with a little melted fat run on the top.

HERRINGS AND HORSERADISH PASTE

2 cooked herrings.
1 oz. grated horseradish.
1 tablespoon milk.

2 teaspoons vinegar.
1 teaspoon sugar.
A little salt.

Remove the skin and bones from the fish and flake the flesh carefully with a fork. Put in a basin, add the rest of the ingredients except the milk and mix thoroughly. Then add the milk gradually, stirring well with a wooden spoon. The mixture should be just thick enough to spread on the bread. Butter will not be needed for these sandwiches.

HARD ROE BUTTER

Boil a hard herring roe or two for a few minutes in salted water. Drain, then mash or pound it. Add pepper and salt, a few drops of vinegar, and a very little softened (not oiled) margarine. Beat together and press into little jars ready to use for the lunch basket.

SAVOURY ROLLS

4 oz. minced chopped meat.
4 oz. breadcrumbs white or brown.
1 tablespoon of seasoning, i.e.

Worcester sauce, tomato or mushroom ketchup.
1 cold potato.
1 teaspoon dripping

Mix together thoroughly, fry in a flat cake in a pan brushed with dripping, lightly browning on either side.

When cold, cut into fingers and roll each one in a slice of wheatmeal bread lightly spread with margarine. This is a change from sausage rolls made with pastry.

A fish mixture may be made instead.

HAY-BOX COOKING

PROVIDED that the dish has a good start on the stove and is simmering when packed into the hay-box, it will complete its cooking perfectly.

Naturally, the cooking takes longer, but no attention is needed. Workers who use a hay-box can return home to find a hot meal almost ready for them.

To make your hay-box, choose a strong packing-case with a lid, or a tin box with a hasp lock. Even an old trunk will serve the purpose. Line it well with clean newspaper ; cover the lining with clean felt or old blanket if you have it ; if not, with more newspaper. Follow the same procedure with the lid, padding it well. Then fill the box with clean hay. If you have a lawn you can make your own hay from the cuttings.

Make a hay cushion 4 inches deep, to fit the inner section beneath the lid.

Arrange the hay in tight packing to reach within 4 inches of the top. Part the hay to make a nest for each pan. Short-handled pans with tight-fitting lids are best. Space the nests 4 inches apart. The number of nests that you can manage depends, of course, on the size of the box. Fill the pans with boiling water ; put on their lids and place them in the nests. Cover with the cushion and leave for some hours. After this, the nests will keep their shape for the pans.

TO USE THE HAY-BOX

Bring the food to the boil in a saucepan on the stove. Secure the lid tightly, then wrap the pan quickly and compactly in newspaper before you place it in the nest. Cover it with the cushion and fasten down the lid. Do not open the box again until the cooking is completed. After the dish is removed from the hay-box, reheat for a few minutes. This is especially necessary after a long period of cooking, as for porridge or a stew.

Here are a few cooking times to which you should refer when using a hay-box.

Time-table for a Hay-box

	On the Stove.	In the Hay-box.
Vegetable soups (dried pea, etc.)	45 mins.	4 hours.

	On the Stove.	In the Hay-box
Potato or root vegetable soup	15 mins.	$1\frac{1}{4}$ hours.
Plain meat stew	30 mins.	$3\frac{1}{2}$ hours.
Meat pudding	45 mins. (boiling)	3 hours.
Oatmeal porridge	5 mins.	6 hours or overnight
Stewed rice	2-3 mins.	$2\frac{1}{2}$ hours.
Stewed dried fruit	2-3 mins.	$3\frac{1}{2}$ hours.
Stewed fresh fruit (apples, etc.)	2-3 mins.	$1\frac{1}{2}$ hours.
Suet pudding	30 mins. (boiling)	$2\frac{1}{2}$ hours.

INDEX

ARTICHOKES, TO COOK, 11-12.
Asparagus, to cook, 12-13.
Au gratin, marrow, 27.
— — spinach, 33.
Autumn vegetable platter (hot), 41.

BACON, FOOD VALUE OF, 5.
— rinds, to use up, 95.
Baked beetroots, 15.
— cauliflower, 20.
— fish and oatmeal balls, 99.
— onions, 30.
— potatoes, 46.
— — stuffed, 51-52.
— rabbit, 84.
— savoury liver, 89.
— stuffed sheep's heart, 93.
— turnips, 36.
— vegetable platter, 40-41.
Bake-house mutton, 81.
Barley broth, 104.
— soup, Polish, 104.
Bay leaf, to use, 65.
Bean salads, 61.
Beans, broad, to cook, 13-14.
— French, to cook, 14-15.
— runner, to cook, 14-15.
Beef recipes, 79-81.
Beetroot and cabbage soup, 103.
— and corned beef, 95.
— recipes, 15-16.
— soup, 103.
Biscuits, potato, 54.
Bloaters, to cook, 73.
Body-building foods, 5.
Boiled potatoes, 45.
— rabbit, 85.
Brain sauce, 115.
Brains on toast, 94.
Braised brisket of beef, 79.
— lettuce with peas, 26.
— onions, 29.
— spinach, 33.
Brawn, to make, 92.
— vegetable, 63-64.
Bread, food value of, 5.
— Irish potato, 48.
— oatmeal, 99.
— potato, 58-59.
— puddings, 112.
— recipes for, 111-114.
— soup, quick, 102.
— stale, to use up, 111.
— to keep fresh, 111.
Bream, grilled, 77.
Brisket of beef, braised, 79.
Broad bean purée, 14.
— — salad, 61.
— beans, recipes for, 13-14.
Brose (oatmeal), 99.
Brotchan Roy (leek soup), 108.
Broth, barley, 104.
— sheep's head, 93.

Brown bread, 113.
Brussels sprouts and celery, 35.
Butter, food value of, 5.
— hard roe, 122.

CABBAGE SOUPS, 103, 108, 109.
— recipes for, 16-19.
— red, casserole, 18-19.
Calcium in the diet, 9.
Calories, meaning of, 7.
Caper sauce, 115.
Capers, substitute for, 68.
Carrot and oatmeal soup, 105.
— and potato purée, 154.
— beehive, 23.
— casserole, 22.
— croquettes, 21.
— pudding, uncooked, 21.
— recipes, 20-23.
— roll, 22.
— sandwich filling, 20.
Carrot-cap salad, 55.
Carrots, food value of, 6.
— grated, as sandwich fillings, 121.
— to cook, 20-23.
Carton meals, 120.
Casserole, Dutch (vegetable), 40.
— of beef, 80.
— of fish, 74, 75.
— — with herbs, 75.
— of red cabbage, 18-19.
— of swedes, 35.
— savoury carrot, 22.
— supper (vegetable), 49-50.
Cauliflower, recipes, 19-20.
— salads, 60.
— soup, 106.
Celeriac and potato salad, 63.
Celery and Brussels sprouts, 35.
— and cabbage soup, 108.
— leaf salad, 62.
— recipes, 23-24.
— relish, 62.
— sauce, 115.
— soup, 106.
Cereals, food value of, 5.
Champ, 29, 53.
Cheese, food value of, 1.
Chervil, 66.
Chicken, tough, to cook, 87.
Chicory salad, 63.
Children, food for, 7, 9, 72.
China Chiloe (meat recipe), 82.
Chinese fish dish, 75.
Chives, 66.
Christmas pudding, 59.
Cod steaks, crumbed, 76.
Confectionery, food value of, 5.
Corned beef recipes, 94-95.
Cow heel with parsley sauce, 90.
Creamed cabbage, 17.
— celery, 24.
Creole soup, 109.